IN SEARCH OF
SHERGAR

COLIN TURNER

SIDGWICK & JACKSON
LONDON

First published in Great Britain in 1984 by
Sidgwick & Jackson Limited

Copyright © 1984 Colin Turner

Picture research by Philippa Lewis

ISBN 0-283-99065-1

Printed in Great Britain by
The Garden City Press Limited, Letchworth
Hertfordshire SG6 1JS
for Sidgwick & Jackson Limited
1 Tavistock Chambers, Bloomsbury Way
London WC1A 2SG

To my mother, who taught
me to love animals, and
to all horse lovers

Author's Acknowledgements

My thanks to Norman Hartley and Vanessa Young, without whom the book would have been impossible. Also to my colleagues at IRN and LBC for their great help and assistance; to the many members of the Shergar syndicate who encouraged me to continue my investigation; to the personal friends all over the world who had to put up with me and my highs and lows; to 'Judy', and all the people I had to use as cover on my many trips over the months; to the photographers who gave me photos for the book; and, finally, to the many others who helped, but for obvious reasons cannot be named, and to all those mentioned in the book who, in one way or another, tried to assist and encourage me in my search for Shergar.

Preface

Just after 8.30 p.m. on the night of 8 February 1983, a group of vehicles, driven by armed, masked men, entered the gates of Ballymany Stud, near Newbridge in County Kildare – one of the two stud farms in Ireland owned by the Aga Khan. There were no guards on the gate and the vehicles drove unnoticed through the darkness up the long, winding drive to the small cluster of barns and cottages at the centre of the Stud.

At least two of the men knocked at the house belonging to Jim Fitzgerald, the head groom at Ballymany. Bernard, the Fitzgeralds' twenty-one-year-old son, came to the door, and as soon as he opened it the men threatened him with the snouts of their machine-guns, then pushed past him and found Mrs Fitzgerald in the living-room with six other members of her family. Jim Fitzgerald heard the commotion and came running from another part of the house – straight into the masked men and their machine-guns.

The gun-men told Fitzgerald that if he did not co-operate his family would be killed. They locked Mrs Fitzgerald under guard in one room, with her two young daughters and her five sons. Then they took Fitzgerald outside and forced him to take them to the stallion barn and identify Shergar – the prize of Ballymany – the superhorse who had gone there to stand at stud, after being syndicated by the Aga Khan for ten million pounds, at the end of a brilliant racing career.

The next morning the Irish police, the Garda, issued only a brief statement. It said that the dual Derby winner, Shergar, had been stolen at gun-point and a two-million-pound ransom had been demanded for his return. The ransom demand had been given verbally to Jim Fitzgerald. The Garda said that after Fitzgerald had been forced to point out Shergar's box, the gun-

men had led the horse out, loaded it into a horse-box, and made Fitzgerald lie face down on the floor of one of the vehicles with his face covered by a coat. Four hours later, after being driven around blindfolded, Fitzgerald was released along the Naas dual carriageway, about seven miles from the Stud.

The news shocked the racing world and horse lovers everywhere. Headlines screamed: 'SUPERHORSE SHERGAR KIDNAPPED'; 'DERBY WINNER SNATCHED FROM STUD', but though the stories were told in massive type, there were very few details.

Then, on 10 February, there were new headlines: 'SHERGAR KIDNAPPERS REPEAT THEIR £2 MILLION RANSOM DEMAND'. The Garda had confirmed that direct contact had been made between the kidnappers and the French manager of the Ballymany Stud, Monsieur Ghislain Drion, who looked after the Aga Khan's racing interests in Ireland. The demand had been repeated in a phone call to the stud.

The Garda released no further information, but it was obvious to a stunned outside world that they had no clues whatever as to the whereabouts of Shergar. The unthinkable had happened. In horse-loving Ireland, the superhorse had vanished. . . .

Chapter 1

'Hello. Is that the sports desk?'

'Yes.'

'Is that Colin Turner?'

'Yes. Colin Turner speaking.'

'Are you interested in finding Shergar?'

'Yes, of course I am. Why?'

'Don't ask too many questions. I can't talk for long. Give me a number where I can contact you.'

'You already have this one at LBC,' I said.

'No. I want to talk to you without it being recorded.'

'It won't be recorded . . .'

There were some clicks, then the line went dead. That was the end of the first call from the anonymous voice and, though I didn't realize it at the time, the beginning of my search for the superhorse, Shergar.

The first call came at about 1.40 p.m. on Saturday, 12 February – the third day after Shergar had disappeared. Half an hour before, I had finished my regular Saturday racing preview for listeners to the local radio station, LBC, the London Broadcasting Company. Since 1975 I've been the racing consultant and sports commentator for the Independent Radio News, the news service which serves LBC and forty-four other local radio stations throughout Britain. I've been a horse lover and a racing enthusiast all my life. Before IRN, I worked in the United States, as a freelance sports broadcaster, based in Boston. Unlike some racing people, I also love horses as animals, as well as enjoying the excitement of the sport. I mention that because it was something that was going to bind me to the mysterious voice, even when all my other instincts told me to have nothing

1

to do with him because he was leading me into dangerous and unpredictable waters.

This love of animals goes right back to my childhood in Ireland. The first thing I rode was a pig. I fell off, of course, but I graduated later to goats and donkeys and, finally, to my first pony. By the time I was twelve, I was riding seriously, taking part in local shows and gymkhanas around Cork. But the competitive riding ended when I fell off and broke my collar-bone, and I decided to stick to hurling and football! I still ride for pleasure whenever I get the chance.

I started out in broadcasting quite young, too. At the age of fourteen-and-a-half, I wrote to the Irish national radio station, RTE, and told them I wanted to broadcast. They invited me to their studios, but I was very cross because they showed me round and offered me tea and cake when what I really wanted to do was to get on the air! A year later, when I was fifteen, I did manage to make a start at RTE, with a small job on a junior sports programme for young listeners. After that, I stayed in sports journalism – in Ireland, in the United States, and then in Britain with IRN/LBC. I cover most sports, but racing is my first love and I've had more than my share of success as a tipster – in fact, I managed to make the *Guinness Book of Records* by tipping 264 winners in sixty-four days in 1974, a world record.

The voice made the call in response to something I'd said during the lunch-time sports broadcast. I'd begun, as I always do, with a survey of the day's racing. The meeting at Newbury had been called off because of bad weather and I'd been talking about the horses running at Ayr, and Leopardstown in Ireland. Then Jeff Stelling, who was presenting the programme, asked me about Shergar. He knew I'd been in Ireland on the day of the kidnap and that I'd followed the story at first hand practically from the the first moment, and he asked me to sum up for the listeners the situation as it stood three days after Shergar's disappearance.

The reality was that not a lot had happened since the kidnap itself. Even three days after the kidnap no one knew what was really going on, so I told the story of the kidnap, as it was known at the time from press reports and statements made to the press. It was a very sketchy outline and at the end of my broadcast I made an appeal to my listeners to call me if they had any

2

information that might help with the investigation. The first such caller was the mystery voice, and I didn't take it very seriously. As we sat round afterwards in the news-room in the LBC studios in a small square tucked away behind Fleet Street, I joked with colleagues over a coffee and told them that some nutter had heard my appeal and had called me up but wouldn't say anything. Then I got down to work. For a sports broadcaster, Saturday is the busiest day of the week and I didn't have time to worry about mystery callers.

He called back almost exactly an hour later and he could hardly have picked a worse moment. I was right in the middle of my afternoon programme and I didn't need any interruptions, especially from cranks who liked to call in and then say nothing. I did take the call though, and I noticed straightaway that his voice sounded very scared.

'Are you recording this?' he said, urgently. Then he repeated it and he sounded very agitated.

I asked him what he wanted and he said yet again, 'You mustn't record this.'

I said I wasn't recording and asked what he wanted.

He said, 'I can get you information about Shergar, but I don't want to ring you there.'

I told him I didn't have time to waste playing silly games. I said I wasn't recording and he could go ahead and tell me what was on his mind.

He still wouldn't say anything and eventually I said, 'Look. If you want me to take you seriously, tell me something the police and the newspapers don't know. Just one thing.'

The caller hesitated, then he said: 'I can tell you something about the horse-box.'

'What about the horse-box?'

'No,' he said. 'I can't talk to you here. I'll call you at home.'

'No,' I said. 'I don't give my home number to anyone just like that.'

I was getting really impatient by this time. I wanted to hear what he had to say but I was busy and I still didn't know whether to take him seriously or not.

Eventually, I said, 'Look, if you've got something interesting to tell me, call me after I come off the air tonight. I'll be out of the studio at 6 p.m. I'll give you five minutes. If you don't call in five

3

minutes, I'll treat you as a screwball.'

'All right,' he said, and hung up.

Even though I was busy, I couldn't help thinking about the call. I knew I couldn't have got the man to talk then and there and I wondered briefly whether I should have given him my home number, but so many cranks call into a radio station and I learned long ago to try and keep that kind of call strictly in the office.

During the afternoon, I prepared and checked racing results and, inevitably, talked about Shergar. There aren't many horses that you can talk about easily with people who are not racing fans, but there are a handful that everyone is aware of, and Shergar is one of them. In the public's mind, he really was a superhorse. In 1981, he'd been one of the most convincing winners ever of the Epsom Derby and he had matched that victory with an equally impressive win in the Irish Sweeps Derby. In the last few days the papers had been full of his exploits – with racing commentators writing articles that sounded depressingly like obituaries – and everyone had been reminded that Shergar had won nearly half a million pounds in prize money, but my memories of the horse were much more direct and personal.

The first time I saw Shergar was at Newbury racecourse on 19 September 1980. He was a two-year-old sired by Great Nephew and there had been a bit of talk about him. People were saying that his owner, the Aga Khan, had a potential winner. That afternoon, he ran in the Kris Plate, with Lester Piggott up, and won fairly easily, taking a prize of £2,560. Looking at him in the paddock afterwards, he seemed like any other two-year-old, a bit more striking than most because of his famous white socks and the white blaze on his head, but really he was like a big baby, looking around at everything, wanting to see what was going on. He looked as if he could become a very useful racehorse, but he was still young and inexperienced and his talent unformed.

In his only other race as a two-year-old, Shergar was beaten by two-and-a-half lengths by Beldale Flutter in the William Hill Futurity Stakes at Doncaster on 25 October.

What a difference a winter under that great trainer Michael Stoute made! He ran six times in the 1981 season, and when I saw him at Sandown Park on 25 April, I was really impressed.

Now, he was no longer a baby. He was more cocky, more sure of himself; he seemed to know what the racing game was about; he knew what to do. At Sandown, he had a really impressive win in the Guardian Classic Trial, with Walter Swinburn riding. I know Walter very well – like me, he's Irish, and the Irish tend to stick together in the racing business – but when we chatted about Shergar after the race, he was very cautious. I said I thought Shergar looked a pretty useful animal and Walter just said, 'Yes'.

But I'm sure he knew that he was riding something very special. On 5 May, Shergar ran at Chester and had an even more convincing win over twelve furlongs in the Chester Vase. He just ran away and murdered everything in the race, so it was hardly surprising that by the time the Epsom Derby came round, it was beginning to look like a one-horse race. For a few days before the race, Lester Piggott grabbed some of the headlines because he was riding another top-rank horse, Shotgun, but most of the talk was about Shergar.

It was at the Derby that I decided that Shergar was an even greater horse than Grundy, the 1975 Derby winner, who had always been my favourite up till then. Grundy was the Rocky Marciano of racing: a tough powerhouse of an animal, a roughneck who simply couldn't bear to have another horse get ahead of him, and who hated to lose.

Shergar was quite different. His power was more graceful. Grundy always seemed to be scrapping against all comers, but Shergar gave the impression that he was aware he was the best and didn't need to exert himself to the full to take care of the opposition. In the Derby, once Walter Swinburn came down the hill and around Tattenham Corner and pressed the button, that was it. It was Shergar's race with no one else in sight. Glint of Gold came second and his jockey, John Matthias, admitted afterwards that when he passed the post he thought he'd won. Shergar took it with the biggest winning margin in the history of the race, and it was only when Matthias was reining in Glint of Gold to pull him up that he realized there was another horse – Shergar – in the distance ahead of him!

My strongest impression of Shergar, though, was in the winner's enclosure afterwards. I'd never seen a horse look so sure of himself. Apart from his white markings, the most striking feature of Shergar was his head. It was like a huge Roman head and he carried it in such a cocky way, you had to smile. That Derby day, he made me think of my days as a youngster in the dance-halls in Ireland. You know how it is. You go into the dance-hall and you catch sight of a really pretty girl and you comb your hair and spend a little time plucking up courage to go and talk to her and, just as you're about to walk across some smooth, handsome, confident, young man glides over and takes her away from you as smooth as silk! That's the kind of cockiness Shergar had. In the paddock after the Derby he was looking around as much as to say, 'Well, we took care of that without too much trouble. But then, what did you expect?'

At LBC, we talked on and off about him through most of that Saturday afternoon. I finished my sports broadcast and I came out of the studio at 6 o'clock. Just before five past six, as I was preparing to leave the studios, the voice called again.

He started straight in with his worries about the call being recorded but I cut him off and asked, 'Look, what have you got to tell me? You said you'd tell me something that nobody else knew.'

'It was a double horse-box,' he said.

'Is that all you're going to tell me?'

'It was blue,' he said. 'Irish people would call it a greeny-blue.'

'How do you know this?' I asked.

'Don't ask questions like that.'

'You could be some sort of nutter, for all I know,' I said. 'Why the hell should I believe you?'

'You can check whether it was a double horse-box,' he said. 'And you can find out if it was a greeny-blue.'

'And when I find out,' I said, 'what am I supposed to do with the information?'

'You will know then that I'm right and you'll believe me,' was all he answered.

'All right,' I said. 'I'll check it out. But tell me something else. Is Shergar O.K.?'

'Yes,' he said. 'He's alive and well.'

'Good. I'll check what you've told me.'

'Can I phone you at home?'

'No,' I said. 'I don't give my home phone number to any

6

Tom, Dick or Harry.'

'When can I contact you, then?'

'I'll be in the studio all next week.'

'I want to talk to you tomorrow,' he said.

'All right,' I said. 'I'll come to the studio tomorrow.'

I decided suddenly that the voice had better have a name. A lot of people call me at the studio and leave messages, and an anonymous caller is liable to be ignored. As he was speaking, I was half watching a television screen just above my head. There are several TV sets in the news-room, and on the one facing the phone I was using there was an ITV programme being presented by a young woman called Sally James.

'You'll need a name,' I said. 'I'll call you James.'

'All right,' he said.

'Tell me,' I asked, 'are you big or small?'

He hesitated for a moment, then he said, 'I'm short.'

'Right,' I said. 'We'll call you James Beag.'

Beag is the Gaelic for small; if he'd said he was tall, I'd have called him James Mor. With a code-name based on Gaelic I knew there could be no confusion. There were already numerous calls to newspapers and the police from people saying they had information. Code-names were all the fashion, and most didn't seem to show much imagination. People were calling the Irish papers and saying, 'This is Arkle', or 'This is Red Rum speaking'. There was no risk of James Beag getting mixed up with that kind of caller.

'So I'll call you tomorrow,' he repeated. 'What time will you be in the studio?'

'I'll be in around 12 noon or 12.30,' I said.

'I'll call you then,' he said, and hung up.

When he had gone, I sat down in the studio for a few minutes thinking about the call, wondering what to make of it. All he had told me was that Shergar was taken out in a double horse-box and that it was greeny-blue. His emphasis on the shade was interesting, and it's certainly true that the Irish are most precise about colours. The voice, though – when I thought about it – didn't really sound Irish. It was definitely an English voice, but with a trace of Ireland in it. There were a few words and intonations he used which suggested someone who had left Ireland a long time ago, but he hadn't said enough yet for me to

7

form any real conclusions. Generally it was a soft voice, but when he wanted to emphasize something it could become sharp, and I discovered later that he was capable of using rough language.

For the moment, all I could do was to try and find out whether his information was worth anything. As far as I knew, no one had mentioned a double horse-box, or talked about the colour, and to find out I decided to make a quick check with someone I could really trust.

As I drove up to my home in Highgate, I wondered which of my contacts I should use. I've made a few friends in the police over the years but I wasn't sure which of them would have quick access to inside information, and I wanted an answer before James Beag called back the next day. I decided to use one of my most reliable contacts – an old friend in the Irish Special Branch – and as soon as I got home, I put a call into Dublin Castle.

Dublin Castle is the headquarters of the Special Branch in the Irish Republic. It's a forbidding, fortress-like building which was once an actual castle. The British used it as their police headquarters long before Irish independence, and it became notorious during the period when the Black and Tans were operating. When Ireland became a free state the Irish police took the Castle over. I called the Castle and was told that my Special Branch contact wasn't in.

I called his home, and a relative said, 'He is on duty, but I think he's just nipped out for a minute.'

I knew what that meant and I put the next call in to the pub where I knew he'd be, and got him straightaway.

Without saying where I had got the information, I asked him if he could find out whether it was true that the horse-box used in the Shergar kidnapping was a double box, and if it was known what colour it was. I don't think he took the call all that seriously. He knew that I would be chasing around after the Shergar story like all sports journalists, and I think he took my call as a very routine favour.

When he called me back, though, later that night, his attitude had changed completely. There was no doubt he was really interested. He told me that the information was correct, and I could tell immediately that I'd given him something that the police didn't expect any outsider to know.

He asked me where in hell I had got the information, and I said off-handedly, 'From some fruit-cake who called me up on the phone.'

'Look,' my contact said urgently, 'do you think you could arrange a meeting with this guy? Could you get him to ring me?'

I just laughed. 'No,' I said. 'He might be a fruit-cake, but he ain't fucking mad. I don't think there's much chance of that.'

I was beginning to sense already that whatever happened as a result of that first phone call, my relationship with James Beag was not going to be as simple as that.

Chapter 2

I began Sunday morning as I always do, by going to get the papers. I like to read both the English and the Irish papers, and I go down to the news-stand in Hampstead and buy a collection of them – all those I know I won't be able to pick up around the studios at LBC. There were the usual routine stories about the Shergar hunt in them, but the only major development was a depressing one: rumours of negotiations with the kidnappers had finally turned out to be an elaborate hoax.

Three of my colleagues from the sporting press, Lord Oaksey of *The Daily Telegraph,* Peter Campling of *The Sun* and Derek Thompson of Independent Television, had flown to Northern Ireland after an anonymous caller 'speaking with a distinct Southern Irish accent', according to the *Telegraph's* own account, had claimed to be holding the horse and offered to negotiate with them as intermediaries. The Sunday papers were now writing the whole business off, though some of them were trying to keep hope alive by speculating that the hoax might at least have been a smoke-screen to cover up real negotiations, but that didn't sound very likely to me.

Was my own caller also a hoaxer? It was certainly possible, but after hearing the reaction of my friend in Dublin Castle I wasn't prepared to write James Beag off, and when I went into the studios that Sunday morning I was, for the first time, actually looking forward to receiving his next call. It came at 12.20 p.m. – a few minutes after I walked into the news-room.

'Did you have any luck?' he said.

I hesitated. 'Yes,' I said. 'I checked out one or two things, but a number of people already know what you told me.'

It was a lie, of course, but I had to try to bluff him. I couldn't let him feel I was satisfied with so little information.

10

'Tell me,' I asked, 'how many vehicles were used in the kidnap?'

'Three,' he said, straightaway. 'A car, a van and a horse-box.'

'Did the car pull the horse-box?' I asked.

'No. That was another car.'

He then started on once again about his fear of being taped, but I brushed it aside.

'Give me the licence number of the car,' I said.

'No, I can't do that. Look, I've got to be quick . . . come on, come on.'

'What do you mean "come on"? Just give me a registration number; just give me some number.'

'I'll give you some numbers,' he said, 'but they're all jumbled up.'

He paused for an instant. 'There's a 4, an 0, a 2 and an 8.'

'All right,' I said. 'I'll check that, too. Now what do you want?'

'I want to know if you believe my story.'

'I don't know,' I said. 'I'm not Hans Christian Andersen.'

'Do you think I know anything about Shergar? About the kidnapping?'

'I don't know,' I repeated.

We then talked some more. He mentioned a few things that didn't mean anything to me at the time – he said, for instance, that the car could have been a Hunter.

'I'm going now,' he said suddenly. 'But Fitzgerald wasn't found in Naas. He was dumped in Kilcock.'

And before I could ask him anything else, he hung up.

Beag's parting shot really brought a completely new element into the mystery. There had been quite a lot of confusion about the details of the kidnap – which was understandable, since the police were being careful not to hinder their investigation by giving too much away. The chief witness, Jim Fitzgerald, had been scared for his life by the gun-men and was saying nothing to anyone – but all the accounts agreed on one point: Fitzgerald had been released by the kidnappers on the Naas dual carriage-way, about seven miles from the Ballymany Stud. Kilcock, I was sure, had never been mentioned. It's a tiny village about twenty miles from Ballymany, just by Maynooth, which is much better known than Kilcock because it is the principal training centre for Catholic priests in Ireland.

There had, naturally, been a lot of speculation about which direction the kidnappers had taken – linked to fears that the kidnap might have been the work of an IRA gang – but the geography of the area didn't make guessing very easy.

The Curragh of Kildare is the horse-racing centre of Ireland. It's a stretch of rolling green land, consisting of a broad plain and areas of trees. It has an army camp on one side and the Curragh Prison – where a lot of IRA prisoners are held, incidentally – and the Curragh Racecourse on the other. Ballymany is one of a large number of stud farms and training establishments there, and it isn't particularly conspicuous.

It stands right on the edge of the racecourse and the gallops that all the trainers at the Curragh use actually start at Ballymany's side-door. Like most stud farms, Ballymany would hardly be noticed by a passing stranger. It had a lot of publicity when Shergar arrived there – the Aga Khan came over to welcome the horse and there were pipe bands playing and a party atmosphere. Now that Shergar had been stolen, there were pictures of Ballymany in all the papers, but they were mostly taken from the air. From the road, all you see is a gate with a sign saying 'Ballymany Stud Farm'.

Just below the Stud, there is a crossroads. If you turn left when you come out of the main gate at Ballymany, you would be on your way to Newbridge, and beyond that to Dublin and the North. If you turn right, within the space of two hundred yards you could take any one of four roads which open up virtually the whole of Southern Ireland. From the information that had been released through the Garda by the time of James Beag's Sunday morning call, it wasn't clear how much Fitzgerald himself knew about where he had been taken.

He had told the police that one of the vehicles used by the gang was an oldish car, possibly a Vauxhall Victor or a Hillman Hunter, and he had also spoken about a van. But at some stage he had been blindfolded, or had a coat put over his head, and forced to lie down for a long period on the floor of a vehicle – probably the van. That experience, combined with the threats to himself and to his family by the apparently ruthless gun-men, had left him a frightened, shattered and disorientated man.

Despite this, Beag's claim that he had been dumped at Kilcock, not Naas, gave me something solid to try to check out.

I decided to make the checks by two different routes. First, I called John Draper, a colleague in IRN who was covering the day-to-day story of the kidnap hunt in Ireland, and asked him to try the car numbers out on the police in charge of the inquiry. I also asked him to try to sound them out obliquely on whether there was any doubt about the story that Fitzgerald had been released on the Naas dual carriageway. Then I called Dublin Castle and had another chat with my Special Branch friend.

I wasn't surprised when Draper called me back to say that he had got nowhere. The police at Naas had said they would try to verify the numbers, but no answer ever came. Nor was there any response to John's inquiries about Kilcock. Luckily, I fared much better with Dublin Castle. My contact said his police colleagues would check on the vehicle registration number. They never did come back with an answer, but my inquiry about Kilcock really stirred things up.

I discovered only much later that the original cause of the confusion was that Jim Fitzgerald had been terrified by what he firmly believed to be an IRA gang. When he was set down by the roadside it took him a while to discover where he was, but when he did manage to find a phone the first call he made was to a relation, who came out and picked him up and took him back to the Fitzgerald home, where Jim made sure his family was all right. The official version – that he had been dropped off in Naas, seven miles from Ballymany – was a deliberate plant to cover his real movements. What mattered from my point of view was that James Beag had been right – Fitzgerald had been dropped at Kilcock and this was a fact that had been kept a very close secret indeed.

My Special Branch contact left me in no doubt that Beag's information about the car and numbers was worth taking seriously, but I still had no idea who he was or what he wanted. Was he a member of the gang? Was he being used by the gang to try and open up negotiations through me? Or was he someone on the fringes of the operation who was trying to make some money for himself? As he hadn't actually mentioned money, I had to consider that he might be trying to pluck up courage to turn the gang in – out of revenge, possibly, or concern for

Shergar – though that didn't seem very likely. As far as anyone seemed to know, no negotiations were going on and, officially at least, the syndicate which owned Shergar, headed by the Aga Khan, had set itself firmly against paying any ransom. The official line was that the racing world could never bow to blackmail. If a ransom was paid for Shergar, then no racehorse would be safe and all stables would have to go in for massive security precautions. The Garda, too, had issued a statement saying they would move to block any attempts to pay a ransom.

Yet Beag did not sound to me like a fully-fledged gang member trying to open the way for talks on ransom. I didn't know what to make of him, but there was no doubt that he was very nervous. He wasn't a young man, to judge from his voice. He sounded mature enough, but he had none of the bold, threatening attitude of a kidnapper who is about to make a ransom demand. My feeling was that he was someone who had some connection with the gang but who wanted, for whatever reason, to start acting on his own.

I admit I was nervous. I didn't fancy dealing with someone who might have links with the IRA, and I didn't want to be caught in the middle of a possible row within the gang. As a journalist, though, I was happy enough to feel that I might have a lead on my colleagues, and as a horse lover, I was determined not to neglect any thread which might lead to the safe return of Shergar.

I decided that it was time for another trip to Ireland to see how the situation looked from close up. I flew over on 22 February and it turned out to be an infuriating and frustrating trip. I managed to see no one of any consequence. I tried to see Ghislain Drion, the Aga Khan's manager at Ballymany, and was refused an appointment. It seemed that the stable management at Ballymany had created a wall of silence around themselves, while I felt sure that more use could be made of the resources of the press in the efforts to find Shergar. The nearest I got to Ballymany then was to stand outside the gate with a crowd of reporters, chatting about the latest rumours – but saying nothing whatsoever about my mystery voice or his mention of Kilcock.

I flew back to London and three days later, on 26 February, Beag called again. I was in the LBC studios, and I took the call in the news-room.

'Have you checked things out?' he asked.

'Yes,' I said. 'I've checked things out. Tell me what you want.'

'Are you sure you're not recording this?' he asked.

'Yes, I'm sure,' I said irritably. 'I've told you often enough. I'm speaking from a crowded room, the recording studios are not here.'

'Do you believe me yet?' he asked.

'I believe you know something, but I don't know who the hell you are. What do you want?'

'At the moment, nothing,' he said. 'But we've been let down and knocked about by those people.'

Improvising as fast as I could, I suggested, 'You mean the Aga Khan and his people at Ballymany?'

'Yes. The whole thing's a mess. They've steered us wrong. It's fucked up.'

'Who's "we"?' I asked.

He did not answer.

'What do you want me to do?' I repeated.

'Nothing yet. I'll contact you. Give me your home number.'

I'd already decided that if he brought this question up again, I would give him the number. But when I did, all he said was, 'But you'll only record me at home.'

I was really angry at that, but I kept my temper. I was afraid he was going to rush off the phone again, so I said, 'Look, let me call you back from a coin-box.'

I didn't think he'd give me his number, but I wanted to keep him talking. He didn't respond. In fact, there was no answer at all, but the coin-box idea stuck in my mind.

'All right,' I said. 'Let's set up a completely safe system. You ring me at home. A certain number of rings. We won't even talk on my home phone, so I can't record it. When you ring the signal, I'll go to a call-box.'

'Which call-box?'

'There's one at King's Cross. I happen to know the number.'

It was pure chance that I did happen to know a call-box number, particularly as I'm not very good at remembering figures. A couple of days before, I'd been at King's Cross Station to meet a girlfriend who was coming down from Edinburgh. When she arrived we had to make a phone call, but we'd run out of 10p pieces and had given our number to that we could be called back. The number had stuck in my mind – it was 837-1644 – and I gave it to Beag. It was in a row of call-boxes in the station.

He seemed to like the idea of the call-box and after a few minutes of discussion we had a system worked out. When he wanted to talk to me, he would call my home number. He would let the phone ring four times, then hang up and call again, this time allowing three rings. Finally, he would make a third call, this time letting it ring only twice. When I got that series of signals, I would go straight to King's Cross and wait for his call. I live about fifteen minutes drive away from the station, so we agreed that he would allow half an hour for me to get there.

He wouldn't tell me any more about what he meant about the people at Ballymany 'fucking things up' but I could feel that he wanted to, and I thought that the new system would finally allow him to muster the courage really to say something. I told him I was going to Ireland again.

'Find out what's happening,' he said. 'I'll contact you when you get back.'

And again the phone went dead.

The Irish trip was another wash-out. I tried dozens of times to get through to Ballymany to arrange to see the manager, Ghislain Drion, but I couldn't even get a call through, let alone make an appointment. Everyone was having the same problems: Drion was turning into a real recluse, a shadowy figure who was being seen less and less. The question of Monsieur Drion's remoteness was to become a crucial issue in the story later on, but at the time, it was only irritating.

I spent a day in Ireland and flew back to attend the William Hill Awards lunch at the Hilton Hotel in London on Thursday (3 March). It's always a great occasion. William Hill, the bookmakers, invite 500 or 600 racing people to lunch and to the presentation of their Golden Spurs Awards to the top racing personalities in flat racing and National Hunt racing from the previous season. I sat with a group of my colleagues in the racing press and, of course, the talk was all about Shergar.

Everyone was getting frustrated with the story because there wasn't really a story, as such. Since the kidnap there had just been a string of wild rumours and hoaxes. People from all over Ireland had called in to the police and newspapers with amazing yarns: one day, Shergar had been killed because he'd injured himself in an accident during the kidnap; the next day, the tale was that his head had been cut off; then another call came in and Shergar was alive and had been seen wandering around some country lanes in Southern Ireland. Some of the crazier rumours were nicely summed up by a cartoon in one of the London papers which showed a milk float being pulled at fifty miles an hour through a sleepy village by a mysteriously fit-looking dray!

But for all the jokes, there was no getting away from the darker side of the situation – and the fears that Shergar was really dead. At the lunch, there were quite a few jokes against the Irish. A couple of peole said, 'Well, Colin, what have you Paddies done with Shergar?' They didn't mean it seriously, but the thought was there in everyone's mind that this was, likely as not, an IRA job. Several people at the lunch knew that I'd been taking a special interest in the story and tried to quiz me about what I knew. Did I have any inside tips? Who did I think pulled it off? I fielded the jokes and the questions, and made sure I said absolutely nothing. If Beag was going to put me ahead of the field, I was determined not to risk giving the game away.

When Beag did call again, though, he didn't carry the mystery forward at all. He called me at home on the morning of Saturday, 12 March, using the code system we'd arranged. He rang in the sequence 4-3-2, and I got into my car and raced to King's Cross. Luckily the phone-box was free and he came through almost straightaway.

'What happened in Ireland?' he asked. 'Tell me what's happening.'

I told him nothing was happening. I told him I'd chased around Dublin and Kildare like a blue-arsed fly and found out sweet nothing, and wasn't it time he started telling me something for a change.

'What about those negotiations that were supposed to happen with the three British journalists who were told to fly to Belfast?' I asked.

'That was a rag stunt by the University students,' he said. 'It was nothing to do with Shergar.'

I'm not sure why, but I said to him suddenly, 'We're going to

17

stop calling him Shergar. Call him "the person".'

The idea that we shouldn't mention the horse's name on the phone had been kicking around in my head for a couple of days. I wasn't enjoying these mysterious phone calls, or the idea that I might be talking to the IRA, and it suddenly seemed safer to cut out the name altogether.

'Now,' I said. 'Tell me at least, is the person well? Is he still all right?'

'Yes.'

'Is he being looked after?'

'Yes. By experts.'

'There's only your word for that,' I said.

Beag didn't reply straightaway. Then he repeated, 'It's being looked after by experts.'

'The only way we could know that,' I said, 'is if you send a photograph. Why don't you send me an up-to-date photo?'

He didn't answer. The line just fell silent.

'Did you hear what I said?'

'Yes, I heard you,' he said, and his tone left no doubt that it was all the answer I was going to get.

'So what's happening?' he asked again.

I was really getting mad, but I could feel that he wasn't going to tell me anything, at least not this time.

'I told you nothing's happening,' I said. 'It's all talk and rumour. And I'm going away next week. I'll be in Cheltenham for the National Hunt Festival. You won't be able to contact me.'

I was going on to say that, therefore, he'd better tell me some more now, but I didn't get the chance.

'That's O.K.,' he said. 'Go to Cheltenham.'

Then he hung up again.

It's not hard to guess that I was pretty fed up when I left the phone-box. The situation really wasn't going anywhere. I went over to the news-stand at King's Cross and the first thing I saw was a big splash on the front page of the *Daily Star* with the banner headline: 'SHERGAR SENSATION. Daily Star World Exclusive'.

I bought a copy and read it. It was an interesting story, but really all it did was to eliminate another possible suspect. The 'exclusive' was an interview with the American racehorse breeder Wayne Murty, who – as everyone in the racing world already knew – was one of the Aga Khan's bitterest enemies. The two men had fallen out over the purchase of fifty-six horses from the bankrupt racing stable of the French textile magnate and financier, Marcel Boussac, in 1978.

When Boussac was about to go bankrupt, he had sold the horses to Murty to help pay his debts. But the liquidators ruled that the horses belonged to the Boussac Estate and not to Boussac personally, and the courts ordered that a new sale had to be negotiated. A deal was finally made between the liquidators and the Aga Khan, and Murty lost out heavily. Murty was furious, claiming that the Aga Khan had 'gazumped him' by using his expensive influence to 'have the rules changed', and had snatched the horses from under Murty's nose.

At one point, Murty was so angry that he staged a Godfather-like demonstration against a French official who had stopped him from exporting the horses. He stormed into his office and flung down the severed leg of a racehorse that had been destroyed. Murty had told the *Daily Star* that he knew he must be the prime suspect in the Shergar kidnapping, and he admitted that if he could have taken Shergar from the Aga Khan during the court fight, he would have done so (though Shergar was already owned by the Aga Khan and was not part of the deal). But he also made it very clear that he was not the kidnapper. A great story – but nothing but a dead lead. I was getting nowhere, but then neither was anyone else.

I decided to put the problem aside for a few days and go off to enjoy Cheltenham.

Chapter 3

We have a saying in Ireland: 'The crack is good'. It means everyone is having a great time, the jokes are flowing freely, there's good talk and a good sense of companionship. Well, at Cheltenham the crack is always good – the Festival is one of the best weeks in the racing year. The finest horses in Ireland are matched against the finest horses in England, which is quite an event in itself, but there is more to the Festival than that. It's a week when real friendships are struck up – the kind that can last a lifetime.

There's one story about Cheltenham that says it nicely. A seven-year-old girl was brought to Cheltenham one year because she was ill and out of school and her parents didn't know what to do with her. She enjoyed it so much that she vowed never to miss it, and for the next twenty years she came every year. Finally, she got married on Gold Cup day, to a man she'd met at a previous Festival, and the reception and first hours of married life were on the racecourse at Prestbury Park.

In 1983 I had a really great Cheltenham week, and one of the highlights was a dinner I went to on the eve of St Patrick's day at the Tara Restaurant in a village in the Cotswolds. It was given by the Durkan brothers, who are the biggest builders in Ireland, as well as being racehorse owners. Bill Durkan is a great mate and I was one of twenty-five guests at the dinner, all racing people from both Britain and Ireland, including some of the leading personalities in the horse scene, as well as a couple of well-known Irish politicians.

As usual, there was no getting away from Shergar. Bill Durkan knew how closely involved I was, and I had had dinner with him at his family restaurant in Dublin on the day after the kidnap. Everyone was asking me what I knew. I didn't say anything, and it was interesting to discover that there – among some of the best-informed people on the racing scene – no one really had a clue to what was going on. Quite a few people said they didn't think the IRA would do that kind of thing. Most thought that the kidnappers were just crooks. One Irish guest said, only half-jokingly, that there were plenty of crooks in Ireland who could have done the job. Then one well-known English racing expert said that it wasn't just the Irish – in all his years in the Sport of Kings, he'd met a hundred crooks in England who could have carried it off!

All in all, it was a great week, but I had barely returned to London when James Beag came back into my life.

It was a Saturday morning again – 19 March. He called me at home, used the code, and I went galloping off to King's Cross Station.

When he came on the line, Beag's first question was, 'Did you enjoy Cheltenham?' Somehow his attitude sounded different from that of the previous calls.

He had never asked me that kind of question before: we didn't exactly have a social relationship, and we certainly hadn't had any amicable chit-chat in our previous conversations! He asked me about Cheltenham almost casually, but there was a touch of menace in the question. It was more like a demand – a question to check up on me, rather than to see how I had been doing. I had the feeling, suddenly, that I might have been followed around Cheltenham, even to the dinner. I thought about all the people I'd met during the Festival week and wondered if any of them could have been James Beag.

I didn't know how to answer, so I just said, 'Sure. I met a lot of people. I had a few laughs.'

Then I dropped a clanger. I said, 'Yes, a lot of people. But I didn't meet anyone with two million pounds to spend for the person.'

It was meant to be a little joke, but it certainly didn't get any laughs.

There was complete silence for a few seconds, then he said in a very cold voice, 'When are you going to Ireland again?'

'I don't know,' I said. 'I really haven't a clue. If something breaks, I'll go, or if my chief editor, Ron Onions, sends me.'

'Could you go on Thursday?' he asked.

21

I hesitated. I didn't know if I'd be able to arrange a trip, but I could feel that this conversation was different from the usual ones.

'Yes,' I said. 'I could go.'

'Right,' he said. 'Fly to Dublin on Thursday. Go to Jury's Hotel in the morning. Wait there. You'll be contacted.'

'Who's going to contact me?' I said.

'Someone will contact you.'

'I'm not going on some fool's errand,' I said. 'What am I going there for?'

'You're going over there, and you're going to be contacted,' he said.

Then he added a curious phrase: 'And it's all for the good.'

Looking back, it seems crazy, but at that moment I really thought they were going to give me Shergar! I suddenly had an image of myself leading Shergar along the Ballsbridge Road by a lead.

'Am I going to meet the person?' I asked.

I meant 'am I going to meet the horse?', but I realized later that Beag had misunderstood me and thought I meant the person I was going to be contacted by.

'I don't know how they'll contact you,' he said.

By this time, I was really scared, as well as being excited.

'I'm not going to use my own name on the trip,' I said.

'When you're in the hotel, you'll have to use your own name,' Beag said. 'They'll be contacting you by name. What if you're talking as though you're Mr Smith, and they try to contact you?'

I had to take the point. 'All right,' I said finally, 'I'll be there on Thursday.'

It didn't take me long to organize the trip. My boss, Ron Onions, was very understanding. He knew I wouldn't use LBC's time unless I thought there was something in it, but my worry was that I might well make the trip and then find out something I couldn't – or wouldn't – use straightaway for LBC.

Anyway, I flew over on Thursday, 24 March, and went straight to Jury's Hotel. I'd arranged to see a few friends as a cover for the trip, and I always enjoy staying at Jury's anyway. The hotel is situated on the main road from Dublin going towards Blackrock, Monkstown and Dun Laoghoire. It's about three miles out of the city centre, in Ballsbridge, one of the most famous areas of Dublin, within striking distance of the Balls-bridge Showground where the Royal Dublin Horse Show has been taking place since the eighteenth century. Jury's is one of the best hotels in the city. It's famous for its Irish cabaret and every summer thousands of visitors come to see the show from all over the world. Then Jury's sends the show on a world tour, with the help of Bord Failte, the Irish Tourist Board. There's always a lot going on in the hotel, and it has some really nice bars and restaurants – the Dubliner Bar, a favourite meeting place of the sports crowd, and the Kish Restaurant, which specializes in seafood.

When I arrived that morning, I bought one of the Irish morning papers and settled down in the Coffee Dock, a general snack bar and morning meeting place.

I didn't order coffee. I had a pot of tea and a plate of delicious brown bread, and settled down to read the paper. At first, I was quite excited. I was sure I was on the point of finding out something really significant; I was also a bit scared and I didn't really know what I was in for. I drank the tea, and read the paper, and gradually the tension slackened off. No one made a move, and there were no messages on the tannoy. I'd told reception I was expecting someone to look for me and had said where I would be, but the paging system covered all the function rooms anyway, and I knew that Jury's was very efficient with messages.

Nothing happened. I bought some more papers. There were a few snippets about the search for Shergar, but no news of any importance. The trail had gone cold and the sports writers were tiring of rumours and speculation. I went on reading, ordered more tea, and still nothing happened. By midday I was becoming really irritable. I'd flown all the way over from London and all that was happening was that I was drinking tea and eating brown bread in Jury's Coffee Dock and beginning to feel more than a bit foolish.

I went on waiting. There didn't seem any point in leaving and, anyway, I had no idea what my next move ought to be. Then, finally, at 12.45, an announcement boomed out over the tannoy system.

'Message for Mr Turner. Mr Turner, please.'

23

I rushed out of the Coffee Dock, trying to stay calm and at the same time hurry, and went down the hotel corridor to the reception desk. The receptionist referred me to the switchboard, and I went round the corner to find two busy women operators in a tiny cramped, switchboard room.

'You have a call, Mr Turner,' one of them said.

I went to the cubicle and said, 'Hello,' into the receiver.

'Is that Colin Turner?'

'Yes. I'm Colin Turner.'

'I'm a friend of James Beag.'

The voice who said 'I'm a friend of James Beag' was quite different from the voice in London, and definitely Irish.

'Are you enjoying your tea and brown bread, Mr Turner?' the voice said.

'Yes thank you.'

It was all I could say. I'd got the message. I'd been watched and inspected. Probably from close-up, while I was sitting in the Coffee Dock. The thought wasn't reassuring.

'Let's talk about the person,' I said.

'Despite the stories in the press that the person is dead, this is not so,' the voice said.

'You mean the person that was reported to have had an accident ten days ago and died of his injuries is still alive?'

'Yes,' the voice said. 'The person is still alive. And he'll be kept alive.'

'Can you tell me anything else about the person?' I said.

'He's being well taken care of.'

'What do you want me to do?' I asked.

'Don't do anything with this information.'

'You haven't given me any information.'

There was a pause, then the voice said in a sharp, angry tone, 'The animal is still alive but we are being pissed about.'

'Look,' I said, 'I didn't come all this way just to find that out. You could have got your other man to tell me that kind of stuff in London.'

'Yes, we could,' the voice said. 'But first, we wanted to get a look at you. We wanted to make sure we were dealing with the right kind of person.'

'And are you satisfied?' I said.

'Yes.'

'So, where the hell do we go from here?' I asked.

'Go to Ballymany, and talk to Drion.'

'That's no good,' I said. 'I've tried that. Drion's not talking to the press. He's not talking to anyone.'

'No,' the voice said. 'He's not talking to us, and if he doesn't, we'll kill the fucking person. That man [Drion] has upset us a great deal.'

'Do you want me to arrange a meeting with you and him?' I asked.

'Drion knows what he has to do,' the voice said. 'When we talked to Drion about money, he slammed down the phone. You go and talk to him. Find out what he has to say, tell him to do his own dealing. If he says nothing, report it in your radio programme.'

Then the line went dead.

I was getting pretty fed up with these calls that ended suddenly with me not knowing what the hell was going on, and this one really got my goat. I hadn't learned anything, except that both my callers obviously had something to do with the gang, and claimed to have been in touch with the Aga Khan's racing manager. But if I did go to Ballymany, Drion wasn't going to talk to me and, anyway, I wasn't at all sure I wanted to be the direct intermediary in talks with the kidnappers. What I'd hoped was that James Beag was someone on the fringe of the gang, someone looking for a reward for information, not a ransom for the horse. Until I was sure which I was dealing with, I didn't fancy going much further. Still, I couldn't just give up. I called a friend and tried to get a private number for Ghislain Drion. I didn't have any luck, so I called the Ballymany Stud number and got the usual endless series of engaged signals. It sounded as though the phone was off the hook, but I couldn't believe they would do that when they were supposed to be waiting for information about Shergar. I stopped trying the number for a while and called a few friends and contacts. Later, I tried again from the GPO in O'Connell Street and, finally, I got through.

A man's voice asked me who I was. I was sure he was a policeman. I said I wanted to talk to Mr Drion.

'Mr Drion won't see anyone, unless he has a name.'

I decided there and then that I wasn't going to give my name.

Why the hell should I get myself into trouble that I didn't understand? If the callers wanted my help, they were going to have to be a lot more frank than they were being. If I did manage to talk to Drion, I could just imagine the conversation. I simply hadn't been told enough to make my approach convincing.

'I just want to leave a message for Monsieur Drion,' I said. 'Tell him to answer his phone, or *the people* – do you understand that, *the people* – won't ring him.'

Then I hung up.

I walked out of the GPO and down O'Connell Street to Eason's Bookstore.

I've been going to browse in Eason's since I was a kid, and it is a good place to think. I love the bookstore, it sells every kind of book, including any sports book I've ever needed, and I can still remember buying books and pencils and little gadgets for school there. I wandered around Eason's for a little while, thinking about the new voice. He was Irish, but not a Dubliner. People from the capital have a special glibby way of speaking and they're inclined to shorten and sharpen words a lot. The Dublin accent is very distinctive – and it's been made famous by a lot of well-known Irish actors, in the plays of Sean O'Casey, for example. No. He wasn't a Dubliner, but that was as far as I could guess. Was there a touch of the North in his voice? Possibly, but I couldn't be sure. There were no very striking characteristics about the voice. It didn't give me any clues.

In Eason's I took stock. I'd been called over to Dublin, spied on – vetted almost – then told some cock-and-bull story about how they couldn't manage to talk to Ballymany. Well, welcome to the club, I thought. No one seems to be able to talk to Ballymany.

But I wasn't ready yet to play pig-in-the-middle – I wanted more to go on and I didn't have it. I walked out of Eason's feeling really depressed. The way it looked then, the whole trip to Jury's had been a complete waste of time.

26

Chapter 4

When James Beag called me again on the Wednesday after my return from Dublin, I went straight into the attack. I was still seething at the way things had gone in Dublin and when he rang my home and used the code, I went to King's Cross all ready for him. When I got to the station, I thought for a moment there was going to be no call. The row of phones where our call-box was located was sectioned off and a team of workmen were preparing to install new equipment. There were already hoardings round several of the boxes but, miraculously, they hadn't got to ours yet.

When Beag came on the line I started slanging him roundly about the Irish trip.

'That was a fine fucking mess you got me into in Ireland last week. Don't ever try to do that to me again,' I shouted. 'In fact, I won't ever put myself in a position where you can do that to me again.'

To my amazement, he apologized.

'I'm sorry about that,' he said. 'I couldn't do anything about it. The whole thing went wrong on the Wednesday night before you arrived.'

He didn't say what went wrong, and when I asked him, he wouldn't tell me. He sounded angry, too, but not with me.

I told him I'd been shit scared in Ireland, which I was, and he said again, 'I'm sorry. It couldn't be helped.'

He obviously wasn't ready to say more, so I asked the usual question. 'Is the person all right?'

'Yes. He's still being looked after.'

'And what about the story in the papers about the photo and the hotel in Howth?'

A story had appeared just after my return from Dublin which

27

said that a current photo of Shergar had been sent to the stable management at Ballymany. According to the reports, it hadn't been sent to the Stud direct, but to a hotel in the Howth area of Dublin, in a packet addressed to Ghislain Drion.

Beag said he didn't know anything about it.

I didn't know whether a photo had been sent or not, but it was certainly possible, and I didn't want to let him off with just a straight denial so I tried to bluff him a bit. I knew the names of a couple of hotels in Howth, so I said, 'You mean there was no packet sent to the Sutton or the St Lawrence?'

He repeated the names of the hotels as I said them, thought for a minute, then said again, 'No. I know nothing about that.'

'Are you sure?' I said.

'Forget all that,' Beag said. 'Something big is going to happen at the week-end.'

I asked him what it was, but he wouldn't give me so much as a hint.

'It's something big,' he said. 'I'll be back and I'll tell you about it.'

As he was talking, there were workmen all along the line of call-boxes. I didn't know exactly what they were doing. They seemed to be installing new telephones and I didn't know if the new ones would have the same numbers as the old ones, so I told Beag what was happening.

'We'd better have a new system,' I said.

I happened to know the number of a call-box I used quite often in Hornsey Lane, in North London, not far from my home. So we left the King's Cross code as it was and added a fourth part of the signal for Hornsey Lane. If he wanted me to go there, he would call four times – four rings, three, then two, then two again.

I was getting pretty nervous during the call. The workmen were unsettling and there was also a policeman walking up and down outside the line of boxes. He kept peering into the one I was using and he was making me feel jumpy. I wanted to break off the call and Beag obviously wasn't going to say anything. I wasn't sure if the policeman knew something, so I hurried Beag through the details of the new phone code.

When he was satisfied, he said, 'Right. I'll call you Saturday.'

This time, gratefully, I was the one who hung up.

He did call on Saturday, exactly as he promised. The only problem was that he'd either forgotten the new code, or decided he didn't want to use it, and he gave me the series of rings that meant I was to go to King's Cross.

He had called my flat at ten past seven in the morning. It was Easter Saturday and freezing cold, and I'd only had time to make myself a cup of tea. So I wasn't in the best of moods when I got to the station, but at least the call-box was still in use, and he came on the line almost immediately.

'This had better be good,' I said. 'It's effing cold and I've only had a cup of tea.'

'Just listen,' he said. 'What I'm going to tell you is the truth. For the past few weeks we've been dealing with a man who was setting up a deal for us with those people.'

'You mean the people who own the product?' I said.

'Yes. That's right. And they agreed to make a payment. Last night, a plane took off from London with that payment on board.'

'Where did it go?' I asked, unable to believe what I was hearing.

'The plane went to the Middle East, but it stopped first in Paris.'

'Was the money taken off in Paris?'

'Yes. But it's gone on somewhere else now.'

He paused and I said, 'Go on. Keep going.'

He still kept silent and I said again, 'Is that all?'

'Yes,' Beag said. 'Now it's up to you to find the rest out.'

'Now, you just hold it,' I said. 'I didn't drag myself out of bed to come and listen to crap like that. You tell me some more.'

'All right,' he said. 'The plane was bound for the Middle East. The flight number was 208. And there was something else. It was delayed so the payment could be put aboard. The banks hadn't got it ready. It was supposed to take off at 8.30. It left twenty-seven minutes late.'

In the coin-box I was furiously making notes, and trying at the same time to work out how to make him say more about who paid the money and where it had gone to. But he didn't give me a chance.

'Right, I've got that,' I said. 'Now . . .'

'I'm going now,' he said, and once again the line went dead.

29

By the time I got back to my flat it was ten past eight. I switched on the electric fire, made myself some more tea and wondered what to do. I had a very busy day ahead of me, with all the Easter sporting events, and a full schedule of broadcasts. I couldn't afford to spend all day checking up on mystery flights. I decided it was time to get some help from colleagues at IRN.

I called the news-room and talked to Steve Gardiner, who was news editor that day. Steve is a huge chap, six feet four inches tall, and very efficient and professional. I told him something was happening on the story I was on – I didn't need to spell it out, he knew I was hunting for Shergar – and could he check with Heathrow about a flight that was supposed to have gone out on the previous night to a Middle Eastern destination. I gave him the flight number, 208, and he said he would check and ring back. He didn't ask me any questions. He knew the story was important and that was enough. He called back fifteen minutes later. He'd checked with Heathrow and there was no flight of that number and nothing to a Middle East destination at around that time.

'O.K.,' I said. 'Could you check Gatwick for me?'

It was much easier to have the desk do it for me, because they have all the contact numbers in the news-room, and a list of people to call if they have any special problems with a query. When Steve called back, it was with the same news: nothing at Gatwick either. I really cursed Beag. I'd been sold another dummy.

'Look,' I said to Steve, 'could you make one more check? Could you call Gulf Air and find out from their London office if they had any flights out last night that might fit?'

Steve was getting busy himself by then so he passed the query on to one of our young reporters, Joanna Crosse, who has since gone on to become a news reader. She called Gulf Air and drew another blank.

Then Derek Grant came into the picture. He was also on duty that morning, as week-end output editor, and I asked him to give a hand as well. Derek is an East-Ender, with years of experience as a reporter. Once he starts something, he doesn't easily let go. Without giving away too much of what Beag had said, I told him I was sure this plane existed but no one seemed to have any information about it. A little while later Joanna called back, just as I was having a shower. Neither of them had come up with anything. I cursed Beag, and was just about to go back into the shower, when the phone rang again. I stood in my bedroom, dripping wet and listened to Beag's coded series of signals. He wanted me again at King's Cross.

I was livid. I phoned Steve Gardiner and said there were developments and I would be late into the studios. Then I raced up to King's Cross and, believe me, by the time Beag came on the line I was really boiling.

'What do you think I am: a bloody fool?' I yelled into the receiver. 'What sort of story is this you think you're telling me on an Easter Saturday morning?'

'Look,' he said. 'I gave you some wrong information.'

'You certainly did,' I said. 'The whole thing was a load of shit.'

Beag ignored my yelling at him.

'I came back to tell you about the money,' he said. 'It was taken from three banks in the City. One of them was an Arab bank.'

'You don't know anything,' I shouted at him. 'I'm going to stop listening to you. You don't know a God-damn thing.'

'Yes, I do,' he yelled back. 'I've got my ear to the ground. I know what's going on. I know all about the meetings that are going on.'

'What meetings? You don't know anything about any meetings. There's no plane. The plane doesn't exist. There's no money. It's just a load of crap like the trip to Ireland was.'

'No, no, it's not', he said. 'I can even tell you about three Arabs who went to see O'Brien [Vincent] and Sangster [Robert] this week.'

'What Arabs?' I said. 'They don't exist. Same as the other things don't exist.'

'They do. They do exist. Three Arabs went to Ballydoyle this week. You can check on that. You'll find out it's true.'

'I suppose I'll have to check this out before I find out whether the money exists, and the effin plane.'

'Yes,' he said. 'They do exist.'

'Oh that's just great,' I said. 'You tell me you know where the money came from but there was no plane to take it anywhere.'

'Yes there was,' Beag said firmly. 'There was no mistake

about that.'

'Do I have the right flight number?' I said. '208?'

'Yes. That's the right number.'

'Then it doesn't bloody well exist,' I said.

'Yes it does,' Beag said. 'They're lying to you. They know all about the aircraft, but you'll have to kick them up the arse.'

'Jaysus,' I said. 'You can't just leave me hanging on a sticky rope like this. Can I talk to my duty editor about this?'

I already *had* asked him, of course, but I wanted to get Beag's reaction.

'Can I ask the police? How about if I ask Superintendent Murphy, who's in charge of the investigation in Ireland. Will he know?'

'Have you checked with the airport?' Beag asked.

'Yes.'

'Have you checked with Gulf Air?'

'Yes. I did that, too.'

'O.K., O.K.,' Beag said, and he sounded really angry. 'If they're giving you a bum steer, I don't give a shit who you tell. But don't tell them it all. Otherwise you'll get a lump of lead in your head.'

'Oh that's just fucking great,' I said. 'I didn't want to be involved in the first place.'

'You can say a little,' Beag said, 'but not the whole lot. You'd better understand that if you don't want to get shot. I'm going now. Do some more checking.'

And he hung up.

By the time I reached the LBC studios, I was pretty upset. This was turning really nasty and I was getting deeper and deeper in without having the faintest idea what was going on. I'd always known it was a risky business, but being told outright that you're liable to get shot really sharpens up the mind, I can tell you.

At the studios, Steve Gardiner and Derek Grant wanted to know what was going on. I didn't know how much I dared say, so I played my cards very close to the chest, thanked them for what they had done, and asked if they'd help me to make a few more calls to check on this damned flight. But just then, all hell broke loose in the news-room. Suddenly it began to look as though the Shergar story was coming to a climax.

It began with a report from RTE – Radio Telefis Eireann – in Dublin. They reported that they had received an anonymous call saying that if the ransom of two million pounds wasn't paid, the head of Shergar would turn up that day at the reopening of Phoenix Park Racecourse. The track had been closed for more than a year and Easter Saturday was to be the grand reopening. Finding Shergar's head would blight the course for ever.

We started chasing the story, putting in calls to our reporters in Dublin and Belfast. Then the Press Association came in with an even more sensational story. They confirmed that reports were circulating that the threat had been received, but they went even further and said that negotiations had been taking place to pay a ransom to prevent it happening. According to the PA, one-and-a-half million pounds had been, or was going to be, paid, and the horse was due to be handed back on the Monday or the Tuesday after Easter.

No sooner was that story in, than another report came over the wires – this time from Eamonn Malley of Downtown Radio in Belfast. He reported that the hand-over was already arranged and he had heard from his sources that it would happen in a place called Bessborough or Bessbrook.

With everyone in the news-room working flat out, we managed to pull together all the strands for a one o'clock news bulletin. All we could do for the moment was to report all the different versions of the story. There was no proof that any of them was true, but it really did look as though we were on the verge of a really sensational development.

Meanwhile, we were still managing to make some calls to Heathrow, Gatwick and Gulf Air to check again on the mysterious Flight 208. Between us, Steve Gardiner, Joanna Crosse and I must have made fifteen or twenty calls. We asked about Flight 208, or Flight 280, or any other number that's like 208, round about that time of the evening. The answer was always the same. There was no flight with that number, and neither Gulf Air nor any other airline had a departure for a Middle Eastern destination anywhere near 8.30 p.m. I wanted to try ringing a few bank contacts as well to see if anyone knew anything about money being sent to the airport for a special shipment, but it was Easter Saturday and I couldn't get anywhere! Then about 1.40 p.m., five hours after our original inquiry, Gulf Air called back.

Joanna took the call. There had been a mistake, the Gulf Air spokesman said. One of their aircraft had taken off at that time. Gulf Air Flight 208 had taken off for Abu Dhabi.

I was standing beside Joanna when she took the call and she relayed to me what was being said.

'Jesus Christ', I said. 'How can an airline company take five hours to discover that one of their own aircraft full of people exists! Ask them when it finally took off.'

Joanna asked and was told, '8.30 p.m.'

'No,' I said. 'That can't be right. Tell them you know there was a delay.'

Joanna passed on the message.

'They say they don't know anything about that,' she said. 'They say they have no further information.'

As soon as she had put down the phone, I called Flight Control at Heathrow. Mysteriously, they had also suddenly rediscovered Gulf Air Flight 208! I asked them what time it took off.

'At 20.30, Sir.'

'No,' I said. 'You're wrong. I believe it left late.'

There was a long pause, then the man – who wouldn't give his name – said, 'Yes. You're right, Sir. I understand it took off at 20.57.'

It was unbelievable. They had taken five hours to 'find' the missing flight and when they did, the information showed that James Beag was right on the nose – down to the last minute. In the middle of everything else that was happening, I'd discovered definite proof that James Beag was telling me the truth.

If he was right about that, I thought, what else was he right about? I had no way of judging which, if any, of the stories flooding into the news-room was true, but if Beag was right, and negotiations had been going on, then I couldn't rule out the possibility that the other part of the story was true and Shergar was about to turn up again.

I didn't want to get left behind – especially on a story I'd followed as closely as this one – and I decided it was time to pull all the stops out and go straight to Superintendent Jimmy Murphy – the police officer in charge of the Shergar investigation.

At that time, I didn't know Murphy personally at all. Later I was to come to know him very well, but on that Easter Saturday

34

I was just another journalist – though I was Irish and I'd a pretty good idea he would know who I was.

Before putting a call through to him, I had a word with one of the senior people at LBC – the week-end editor, Philip Bacon. He agreed that I should make the call and, at my suggestion, he came with me to the studio when I tried to contact Murphy, first at the police headquarters in Naas, and then at his home.

Superintendent Murphy was easy to talk to and I felt able to put my questions to him very directly. I wasn't as direct, though, about my sources. I wanted to let him know I'd been receiving what could be some very hot information, but that I couldn't reveal the full details of the source, especially on the telephone, so I went about that side of things a little cagily.

'Superintendent Murphy,' I said, 'there are a couple of things I have to say to you regarding our Shergar story. Some people have been contacting me for the past couple of weeks and they claim to know what's been going on. They rang me last Wednesday, and they came back again this morning, and they told me that a ransom had been paid. In fact, they told me much the same story as the one given out by RTE. Is there any truth at all in these stories?'

Superintendent Murphy was sceptical. 'I did hear today that there was supposed to have been a ransom paid at 5 a.m. this morning, on condition that the animal was returned on Tuesday morning, but there's no way I would accept that kind of a deal. Unless they're daft altogether, no one would pay out a ransom today with the horse Shergar to be returned on Tuesday.'

That looked like a dead-end, at least for the moment. Some of that hadn't come from Beag, anyway, but I was mixing up my sources a bit, so as not to give too much away to Murphy. I decided to turn next to some information Beag himself had given me.

'Superintendent,' I said. 'Do you know anything about Mr Robert Sangster and Vincent O'Brien and three Arabs holding a meeting at Ballydoyle this week?'

'No,' Murphy said. 'Nothing.'

'Well, I can tell you,' I said, 'that according to my inform-ants, three certain Middle Eastern gentlemen did pay a visit to Ballydoyle and started negotiations there. Have you anything at all to back that up?'

35

'No.' Murphy said.

'Is it possible for you to check it out?' I asked.

'Yes, I could check that out.'

I then went on to tell him the story of the mystery Flight 208. I told Murphy about the calls we had made to the airports and to Gulf Air and how it had taken five hours for anyone to admit that the flight existed.

Then, once again deliberately mixing up information I had got from Beag and from various media sources, I said, 'My information is that the plane left late – twenty-seven minutes late – because it collected a special package, and that package happened to contain half-a-million pounds. It was taken to Paris even though the plane was on its way to the Middle East. I was informed that the money – part of the ransom money – was collected from three Middle Eastern banks here in London yesterday and put on board the plane for Paris.'

Murphy replied that he had no information on this at all, but he agreed to check it out for me.

I went on next to the Belfast story about the horse being handed over in a place with a name like Bessborough or Bessbrook. Murphy knew nothing about that either.

'I think there's a Bessbrook, or something like that, up around Belfast,' Murphy said, 'but I haven't heard of a Bessborough. I'll check that out too.'

Finally I asked him a question for the record. Was he looking for Shergar in Ireland?

'Oh yes,' Murphy said. 'Yes, we are.'

We ended the call with Murphy repeating his promise to check out all the information I had given him, and we agreed we would talk again the next day.

After that, the news-room did begin to quieten down a bit and, mercifully, the first meeting at the new Phoenix Park Racecourse went off without Shergar's head turning up! There was one very curious point, though, which emerged in the news coverage from Dublin. Robert Sangster, who is one of the owners of the track, failed to turn up for the inaugural meeting, once again fuelling speculation that he might just be engaged in negotiations over Shergar. For the moment, though, there was no way of being sure.

Next day, Easter Sunday, I called Murphy back as we had

arranged, but the news was all disappointing.

'There's nothing in the stories at all,' Murphy said. 'Nothing at all.'

I then asked him why Robert Sangster hadn't turned up at Phoenix Park the day before. Murphy didn't know. He knew Sangster had been missing, but he hadn't discovered any reason. He had no information on the supposed Bessborough/Bessbrook hand-over, either, so nothing had yet turned up there.

Murphy was also sceptical about any money having been paid over at all.

'It's a difficult thing for anyone to accept that one-and-a-half million pounds would be paid over on the Saturday morning for the release of an animal worth ten million pounds on the Tuesday morning. That would be taking a very great risk.'

'What if it was half the ransom,' I said, 'or a reward for information?'

Murphy still wasn't enthusiastic.

'I think if any substantial reward was going to be paid,' he said, 'it would have to be on the delivery of the animal.'

For the record, I asked him what the attitude of the police in Ireland would be, if a reward were paid.

'I'd be all against it,' Murphy said. 'I've said that from the outset. There is no way anyone can condone it.'

That was how we left it and, for the moment, there were no developments until James Beag called again on the following Tuesday.

He used our new code this time, and I went to the call-box in Hornsey Lane. I didn't let him take control of the conversation as he always liked to. I went straight in and asked him the question that everyone had been asking me, 'What's all this about money being paid?'

I had told no one about the mysterious Flight 208, but over the week-end the story had started circulating that a ransom had been paid to prevent Shergar's head from turning up at the Phoenix Park meeting. Monday's papers carried denials from everyone connected with Shergar, but it still looked suspicious to me – given what Beag had told me on the last call.

Beag ignored my question. 'Did you find out about the plane?' he asked.

'Yes,' I said. 'There was a Flight 208. You were right. But I found out damn all else. Now suppose you tell me. Was money really paid?'

'Yes.'

'Where did it go?'

'It was taken off the flight in Paris.'

'Who was it paid to?'

'I can't tell you that.'

'Are you telling me that ransom money of two million pounds was paid without the horse showing up?'

'I never said it was ransom money,' Beag said.

'So we're not talking about millions of pounds?'

'No.'

'How much are we talking about?' I asked. '£100,000? £200,000? Half a million pounds?'

'The first two.'

'You mean something like £100,000 or £150,000?'

'Yes.'

'Was it part of the ransom money?'

'You can call it that if you like,' Beag said. 'But it was more like money to keep faith in the situation.'

'Was it paid to keep negotiations open or to keep the person alive?' I asked.

'The latter.'

'So what happens from here?'

'I don't know,' Beag said.

That really annoyed me.

'This is a pretty funny ball game,' I said. 'You own the ball and you don't know what game you're playing.'

I didn't want him just to dry up, so I added, 'So you're saying that the money paid over was confidence money?'

'Yes. It was confidence money so that things can be kept as they are and nothing will happen to the person.'

'So you're happy now. You don't need me any more?'

Beag didn't answer.

I could feel he was about to run off again, so I said, 'That's a lot of money we're talking about.'

Then he said it. For the first time, he came out directly and admitted what his calls were really about.

'I need money too,' he said. 'We all need fucking money.'

38

'Are you not getting any of the money that went to Paris?' I asked, but he didn't answer.

I was still trying desperately to keep the conversation going, especially now that he had finally talked about wanting money for himself.

'Are you saying you want money for information?' I said.

'Yes.'

'Do you mean you want money for the information you've given me up to now, or for what you're going to give me? Or do you mean for the return of the person?'

'Yes. Yes. Yes,' he said irritably. He sounded really agitated.

'I don't know how I'm going to get you any money,' I said. 'I can try. If the person really is still alive, I could go to Ireland and try to get some money. But whoever I ask will want proof. Anyway,' I said, 'what about the reward money that's there already?'

At that time there was a total of £60,000 available for information leading to the recovery of the horse and the capture of the gang. £50,000 had been put up by the Irish Thoroughbred Breeders' Association and *The Sporting Life* newspaper had put up another £10,000.

'That's not fucking reward money,' Beag said. '£50,000. You must be fucking joking.'

'But that's what the reward is,' I said. 'And there's the money from *The Sporting Life* too.'

Mentioning that was a mistake, because it set him off ranting against John McCririck of *The Sporting Life*, who had been campaigning against paying out any money – even though his own paper had put up a reward. Beag had a go at some other journalists too, who had said no ransom should ever be paid. I had to let him go on and wait for him to calm down a bit.

In my own mind, anyway, there was a clear distinction between rewards and ransoms. In the two calls Beag had made since he first started talking about Flight 208, I'd noticed a distinct change of attitude, especially when he was talking about money. At first, when he'd said that money had been paid, he sounded very direct, almost businesslike. He sounded satisfied, pleased with himself, as though something had been achieved. It had crossed my mind that this payment had something to do with what was supposed to have gone wrong on the night before my fiasco at Jury's Hotel. I thought they might have been due to take payment on that Wednesday, before I flew to Dublin, and that the deal had then fallen through and been settled again later – resulting in the payment Beag claimed was made to Paris.

But since the first call, he had been growing more and more irritable. I was pretty sure now that he wasn't getting any of that money, and I suspected he had thought he was going to.

The whole idea of confidence money was mystifying, too. Who had paid it? The Aga Khan? Other members of the syndicate? (The syndicate was formed when Shergar was put out to stud. Previously he had been owned by the Aga Khan.) There were thirty-four owners in the syndicate altogether – many of them a lot less able to bear the cost of losing a large sum of money than the Aga Khan. Had some of them got cold feet and agreed to pay to keep the horse alive? What was equally mystifying was the way the money was supposed to have been paid. It all pointed very much now to an international gang. If it had been a straight IRA job, the money would have been dumped in bandit country in South Armagh. Paris didn't sound like an IRA pay-off point at all.

When he'd calmed down a bit and stopped slanging my good friend McCririck, I decided to try to go on the attack a bit.

'Look,' I said, 'if you want me to get some money for you, there's going to have to be some proof. Tell me this much. Is the person still in Ireland?'

'What made you ask that question?' Beag said irritably.

'Because it's been in all the papers that he may not be. Now, with you asking for money, it'll look as though you're going to run off.'

'You've got to do something,' he said, all agitated again.

'All right,' I said. 'I'll try. I'll go to Ireland. I'll see if I can get some money. I'm off to Liverpool tomorrow for the Grand National. Then I'll go to Ireland, but they'll want all kinds of proof.'

'I've got to go,' he said. 'I've got to go.'

He sounded really agitated now.

'Look, they're going to want proof,' I went on quickly. 'Proof that I'm not spoofing them. I could end up in jail over this.'

'No. You won't.'

'It's great for you to say that,' I said. 'But if the person's outside Ireland, you can't get proof, and I'll be put in jail for collaborating with you.'

I decided suddenly that I would try to wind him up – just to see if I could push him into saying something. I'm very good at winding people up. I often do it in the office and the rest of the staff at LBC get a kick out of it because they admit I'm very good at it.

'If the person is not in the Republic,' I said, almost as though I were thinking out loud, 'how on earth did you get him out?'

Beag didn't answer, so I plunged on.

'You couldn't take him out by plane. All the airports were watched. Anyway, the only person I know who has a plane that could do that kind of job is Vincent O'Brien and he wouldn't do it while he had a breath in his body. Or maybe you just took him over the border? Is that where he is? In the war zone? In South Armagh?'

I still wasn't getting any response, but I went ahead. At that stage, I really didn't have much to lose.

'You could have got him out by sea, of course. You could have taken him out of the ports. Cork, maybe, or Limerick, or Rosslare.'

I was thinking on my feet and I was trying to picture a map of Ireland and list all the ports in order round the coast. I knew I was jumping about all over the place and I couldn't think of any more ports when, suddenly, he said, 'Waterford'.

I was so surprised, I didn't take it in straightaway and just went on with the wind up.

'Sure,' I said. 'Waterford. Plenty of livestock goes out through Waterford. But you couldn't take him out through a big port. Too many rules. Unless everyone's been paid off.'

I didn't say it, but I was thinking that you could very well take him out through Waterford. The port is well-known as an IRA stronghold and quite a few people could be paid – or pressured – into looking the wrong way.

'If you're saying it was Waterford, he must have gone out through one of the little fishing ports around there. Helvick Head, Youghal, Dunmore East,' I said.

'Yes,' Beag said. 'Dunmore East.'

I was really thinking fast now. He was as good as telling me that Shergar had been smuggled out through Dunmore East. I'd

41

never been there. The only reason the name had popped into my head was because in a train station in New York State I once met an Irish nurse who came from there and talked a lot about it.

'Look, for Christ's sake, tell me straight,' I said. 'Was it Dunmore East?'

Beag didn't answer, and I could feel that we were going to go back to the old guessing game routine.

'If you go to Ireland, where will you stay?' he asked.

'If I go to Ireland, should I go to Waterford?'

'Yes,' Beag said. 'But in Dublin, where will you stay?'

'I usually stay at the Gresham, Jury's or the Burlington. One of those hotels.'

'The Skylon,' Beag said.

I knew the hotel, though I'd never actually stayed there. It's a rather characterless hotel on the north side of the city, on the road to the airport.

'The Skylon?' I said.

'Yes. Stay at the Skylon.'

'All right,' I said. 'I'll stay at the Skylon.'

'I've got to go. I've got to go,' Beag said.

'You want me to stay at the Skylon?' I said again.

'Yes. If I want you, I'll contact you there.'

Chapter 5

Once again, the LBC management was very understanding about my making another trip to Ireland. I cancelled all my appointments for the following week and explained the situation to Ron Onions. He just grinned, and said, 'Don't forget to bring the horse back with you.'

Then I drove to Liverpool for the Grand National, on Saturday, 9 April, and, yet again, there was no getting away from Shergar. Rumours had been circulating for a couple of days that one or more of the Grand National horses was going to be snatched, in a Shergar-style kidnapping, and by the Friday night there was talk of secret phone calls and threats to owners and the race organizers. Special security had to be arranged and everyone was very uptight before the start of the race. But there was no kidnapping and the day went off very well. Corbière won, ridden by Ben de Haan and trained by Jenny Pitman, the first woman ever to train a Grand National winner.

After the race, I had a chance to interview Lord Derby. The interview had been arranged through the International Racing Bureau, which deals with all the international aspects of horse-racing. Lord Derby was Senior Steward at Aintree and is recognized throughout racing as one of its great statesmen. He's a very shy man, but warm and generous. If his horse loses, he'll be the first to congratulate the winner. He knows racing inside out but I particularly respect him because he loves his horses – which can't be said of everyone in racing. He is also one of the owners of Shergar. He had bought a quarter-of-a-million-pound share in the syndicate when Shergar was put out to stud and, inevitably, when we had finished talking about the day's racing, the interview turned to the missing 'person'.

I asked him if he would sum up for my listeners what he

thought the situation was at this point, and his answer was pretty depressing.

'I can't believe that a horse can go missing in Ireland for two months. I'm very sorry to say that I think he must be dead,' Lord Derby said. 'I hope not, but I'm afraid it's almost inevitable now.'

I couldn't say anything about James Beag, but what Beag had told me about Waterford was very much in my mind. So I asked Lord Derby if he thought it was possible that Shergar had been taken out of Ireland and was alive in another country.

'It would have been very difficult to take him out,' Lord Derby replied. 'I'm not sure how you could have done it. If he'd been taken out by aeroplane, it would be bound to be known. Air traffic control would have realized there was some unscheduled flight. He could have been taken out by boat, but even that's not very easy. It's quite hard to get a stallion on a boat and you've got to get the right sort of boat to start with. I think someone would have known, if it had happened.'

I couldn't very well say much more, without giving away my special interest in Waterford, so I asked Lord Derby if it would be possible to disguise Shergar.

'Certainly, you could obliterate the white marks on the horse but I don't think you could disguise the horse so that someone couldn't recognize it by now,' he said.

On the whole, Lord Derby was definitely pessimistic and, as a shareholder, he was able to confirm for me, on the record, that there had been no official contact with any kidnappers or supposed kidnappers.

At one point in the interview, I asked him the straightforward question: 'They haven't contacted anyone officially?'

I received the equally straightforward answer: 'No. They haven't and this is what makes me suspect the horse is probably dead.'

If any confidence money had been paid, then either Lord Derby didn't know about it, or he was bluffing very well.

Lord Derby went on to say that he didn't believe that the kidnapping was the work of the IRA or one of the Irish Protestant groups.

I decided it was time to sound out his reaction to the possibility of negotiations.

44

'Lord Derby, what would be your reaction if, for instance, someone contacted you and said they could prove that the horse was alive, say by showing you a picture of him with a Saturday newspaper? Would you still want to negotiate with them, or would you leave it to the police?'

Lord Derby's answer was categoric.

'Well obviously it's a job for the police,' he said. 'And, anyhow, there's no question of paying ransom. From the very first, I've made it clear that to pay ransom would be a total disaster. It would endanger every Derby favourite for years to come.'

I didn't attempt to pursue the point, but Lord Derby had brought it home to me very clearly that if I was to continue with my efforts to get Shergar back, I was going to have to make it very plain to everyone that I was thinking in terms of a reward for information, not a ransom, or even a partial ransom for the kidnappers.

Before leaving Liverpool, I called the Ballymany Stud again and tried to arrange an interview with Ghislain Drion. Once again I was told – this time by a woman – that Monsieur Drion was not available.

However, I did manage to arrange an interview with Jonathan Irwin, the manager of Goff's, the bloodstock dealers and agents, for Monday morning. I very much wanted to get the bloodstock breeders' angles on the Shergar situation, especially since the kidnapping could well have a devastating effect on the bloodstock breeding industry in Ireland, which is worth one hundred million pounds a year, and they might well put up more reward money. I also wanted to set up some interviews in Ireland as partial cover for my trip. Journalists are always very nosey about each other's movements and I didn't want any of my colleagues to know that I was going to be sniffing around Waterford.

That night I took the B & I Ferry, with my own car, to Ireland, and spent most of the Sunday at my family's home outside Dublin, chatting to my mother and sister and, I admit, sleeping a lot to recover from a hectic Grand National day.

On Sunday evening, I moved to the Skylon Hotel. When I checked in I asked if there were any messages and was told, 'Someone called. They didn't leave a name, but they're going to ring back.'

I noticed, incidentally, that the hotel had booked me in the name of Mr Colin Turner, ITV. That often happens. I usually say 'Colin Turner of IRN – that's Independent Radio News, like ITV'. And of course they write down ITV. Eventually, to save argument, I checked in as Colin Turner of IRN–LBC–ITV. It's called covering the field.

I also spent some time working on the other part of my 'cover'. What better reason for going to a place like Waterford, than to spend a few days with a pretty girl? From Liverpool, I'd phoned a girlfriend – let's call her Judy – and she had agreed to take Monday off to come with me. In fact, she stayed with me during the whole Waterford trip, which made it very enjoyable – and provided me with a very solid reason for being in that part of the world. I called Judy from the Skylon, told her I'd arrived and, while I was waiting for her to come over, James Beag telephoned.

I hadn't been sure whether I was going to be contacted by the Irish voice from Jury's again, but when the call came there was no doubt it was Beag.

It was a very quick call. Very snappy and business-like.

'So you're there,' he said.

'Yes, I am.'

'What are you going to do?'

'I'm going to see some people who might help with the investigation,' I said. 'And I'm going to see if I can get an improved bid on your situation. I'm going to see Jonathan Irwin. I might also see Superintendent Jimmy Murphy.'

'What for?' Beag asked.

'I'll talk to who I like. If anyone can help me in any way, I'll talk to them. Anyway,' I said, going on to the attack, 'what was all that shit about kidnappings at the Grand National. All you could hear there was the IRA IRA IRA. If I'm going to talk to people about getting money for you, they'll want to know if it's for an illegal organization.'

He didn't answer straightaway, so I asked: 'Well, are you part of an illegal organization? Or are you part of an international gang?'

'What do you think?'

'I've given up thinking,' I said. 'I'm scared for my life. I

46

don't know who's watching me or who's following me. It's about time you levelled with me for once in your life.'

'What do you want to know then?' Beag said.

'Were they all Irish or not?'

'Only two or three of them were Irish,' Beag said.

'So we're dealing with an international situation?'

'Yes. Now, have I been honest with you?'

'Yes you have . . .'

Then, just as we were beginning to get somewhere, I had to interrupt the conversation. I was talking to Beag from my bedroom, which was at the back of the hotel. It was raining and blowing hard outside but, above the noise of the weather, I suddenly heard some loud banging noises in the yard at the back. I tried to edge towards the window without leaving the phone, but I couldn't see out, and I was really scared. I don't know quite what I expected. I think I had visions of men in balaclavas coming in through the window. I didn't know whether it was going to be the IRA or the SAS, I just felt really scared. Eventually, I put down the phone and looked out of the window. To my relief, all that was happening down there was a couple of hotel staff in white jackets organizing the waste bins.

When I picked up the phone again, Beag said, 'What's wrong? Is someone there?'

'No,' I said. 'There was a noise out the back and I was worried about it. I suppose some of your people are watching me anyhow?'

'No,' Beag said. 'They don't even know you're over there. This is something where we're on our own.'

He said the 'there' quite distinctly. Now I was sure, as I had suspected, that Beag was calling from England. That still didn't explain why he'd insisted on the Skylon Hotel, but at least it was a bit reassuring.

'Well, that's great,' I said. 'Because I don't mind telling you, I'm shit scared already.'

'I will guarantee that nothing will happen to you,' Beag said.

'That's some comfort,' I said. 'What about the other man? The one who contacted me at Jury's?'

'Forget it,' he said. 'Just forget it.'

It seemed to me that there were two groups of people involved, one operating in Ireland and one in Britain. It was

47

possible that the confidence money that went to Paris had been paid to one section of the gang, while another section – which must have involved Beag somewhere – was trying to set up their deal through me. Equally, it was possible that Beag was acting completely on his own and that this was why he had not sent me back to Jury's Hotel, which was familiar ground to at least one other member of the gang.

There was complete silence for a few seconds, so I asked, 'I'm still to go to Waterford, am I?'

'Yes.'

'And I suppose you'll contact me when I get back?'

'When do you return?'

'I don't know,' I said. 'Wednesday, maybe. Or Thursday. I just don't know. It depends on how I get on in Waterford. Am I supposed to see people, or find people, or what? Am I looking for a man? A few men?'

No answer.

'Am I looking for *the* person?'

Again, no answer.

'Am I looking for one person, or for people?' I repeated.

'People,' Beag said.

'If I had my way,' I said, 'I wouldn't be going to Waterford at all. I wouldn't see anyone. I'd disappear to South America if I could. Right now.'

'I'll contact you,' was all Beag said before hanging up.

It wasn't a very promising start to the trip. The only thing I'd established was that it was definitely an international gang I was dealing with, but there was Irish involvement, and Beag hadn't ruled out the possibility that the IRA had some hand in it as well.

My first step was to interview Jonathan Irwin, but I decided that before making any direct approach to him about the possibility of increasing the reward money, I'd talk to him first, on the record, about the situation as he saw it from the bloodstock breeders' point of view. The next day, I drove to Phoenix Park with Judy and did the interview.

Jonathan Irwin is a very popular figure in the bloodstock breeding industry and racing, even though by background and upbringing he was not a 'horsey person' at all. He came late to the bloodstock business but is highly respected as an astute businessman and he is well-known as a raconteur and great teller of Irish stories – something which makes him welcome in every corner of the horse world.

Jonathan Irwin is the Managing Director of the new Phoenix Park racecourse, and he was very keen to promote it outside Ireland as well as at home. He took me on a tour of the installations – the bars and stands and betting arenas – which were still being finished off, even though the track had officially opened. Then I took out my tape-recorder. First, he talked about the track for the benefit of my English listeners. Then, eventually, we turned the conversation to Shergar.

Irwin said he remembered the day of the kidnapping vividly. He'd been in France at the time, and he had thought at first that the story was some kind of practical joke his French friends were playing on him. When he found out that it wasn't a joke, his next reaction had been one of sadness.

'Despite all the political troubles in Ireland in recent years, the racing industry had managed to keep itself apart from all the evil,' he said. 'Now that had changed, and it was very upsetting.'

I asked him what kind of shock it had been for the people in the bloodstock industry, and his answer was blunt.

'It was a hell of a shock for people,' he said. 'We live a very traditional kind of farming life and there's nothing you can do. You can't protect every farm in the country, whether you've got a prize Charolais bull or, as in this case, a thoroughbred stallion. As we know only too well, every country with a democratic background is open to men of violence, to lunatics.

'I don't own any part of Shergar,' he went on, 'but it really was felt very strongly by the Council of the Irish Thoroughbred Breeders' Association that we should stand up and be counted. We wanted to make it well known internationally that there was a reward available to anybody, just to jog their minds. To remind them that they might have been driving down to Newbridge or to Kildare and they might have seen something. Or indeed, there might be people around the country who had seen something.'

I asked him whether it was true that the exact amount of the reward had never been officially divulged.

Irwin acknowledged that it hadn't, and said that he believed it would have been a mistake to set a fixed figure. He went on to say that he felt that a very substantial reward could be made available, well in excess of six figures.

It was an encouraging sign, but I found out later that he had been mistaken and the figure offered by the breeders had never been intended to be higher than £50,000.

I then asked Irwin the same question that I had put to Lord Derby: how did he see the situation now?

Irwin's answer was much more positive than Lord Derby's had been.

'Really, we know nothing,' Irwin said. 'But I think myself that the horse is alive and well and in the island of Ireland. I've no idea where he is . . . but doubtless the people who took the horse have got a horse background, maybe Irish, and that the horse is well protected, either in a large farm in Ireland, or perhaps even underground, perhaps even in a suburb of a city . . . Dublin, Limerick, somewhere like that. A place where people would be least likely to look for a horse of this sort.'

Still with my Waterford information in mind, I asked Irwin if he believed it was possible that Shergar could have been taken out of Ireland.

'I don't think it's likely,' he said, 'although anything is possible. I mean, if you'd asked me six months ago whether a major stallion could be taken, I'd have said I didn't think that was possible. No. I don't think the horse is out of Ireland. It's very difficult to get a horse out of the country. You can dye them. You can do many things to them, but you've got to remember that this is a fit, young stallion. Now if it had just been, let's say, a gelding going over for Cheltenham, or Aintree, sure – nobody would have noticed him. But with a horse like Shergar, the customs officers either this side or on the far side would have remembered, and that hasn't happened. The idea of a ship arriving off Donegal Bay, or of an aeroplane flying into some small landing strip on the West coast and taking off again unbeknown to everybody – that's too far fetched for me.'

I asked Irwin to comment on the fact that the Aga Khan – who was still the principal owner of the horse and the leading figure in the syndicate – had not come over to Ireland since the kidnapping. Wasn't it curious that he hadn't wanted to get directly involved in the investigation?

Irwin said he wasn't really surprised.

'The Aga Khan is a very close friend of mine,' he said. 'But I still wouldn't be in a position to talk about his reaction. I think that people of his background live in a very different world from yours and mine, and from that of most of the listeners. I mean, this man was not only born wealthy, he was also born a spiritual leader, and they are under an awful lot of pressures in many other fields . . . It may seem strange to you and me, but I'm sure there are very good reasons why he has kept out of it, and I'm not quite certain what he would have achieved by holding press conferences at the stud. I think perhaps that when we reflect on it in a couple of years' time, we'll probably see that he has behaved in the correct manner.'

I didn't agree, but I could understand Irwin's viewpoint.

I left that topic and went back to the crucial issue of whether Shergar was still alive. I mentioned that Lord Derby believed the horse was dead and asked him to comment.

'Maybe Lord Derby is a lot older and wiser than I am,' Irwin said, 'and maybe I'm more of an optimist. I just happen to believe that if these people wanted to kill a horse, why didn't they just walk into the box and machine-gun him there and then? I can't see the point of taking him away at great risk to themselves and killing him somewhere else. I think they're keeping the horse to create as much confusion as they possibly can in this breeding season. They're putting pressure on the syndicate. If I could say anything to them, I'd say they've now caused as much confusion to the syndicate and to the mare-owners as they possibly can. They've done as much damage to the Irish nation as they possibly can. If that's what they wanted, then now is the moment they might just start thinking about other people, barring themselves, and come forward and find some way of returning the horse to us.'

Irwin ended the interview with an appeal to anyone who had any information to make an anonymous telephone call to someone in a position of responsibility.

I didn't tell Irwin then about my own anonymous caller. I didn't feel ready to start making any moves on James Beag's behalf. Besides, I didn't share Jonathan Irwin's conviction that the horse was still in Ireland. I wanted some more information – and the most likely place I was going to find it was in Waterford. It had to be the next step.

Chapter 6

The first big hurdle on the Waterford trip had nothing to do with Shergar – I had to smooth Judy's ruffled feelings when she found out that she was being used as a cover! I suppose it wasn't very flattering for her and I had all kinds of plans to break the news to her nice and gently. I certainly didn't want to upset her. She's a really good friend; a very pretty girl and marvellous to be with, but I was going to be so busy in Waterford that there was no way I could disguise the fact that I hadn't gone there just to spend a few days with her. Unfortunately, she found out a little earlier than I intended, so I never got the chance to use a bit of Irish charm.

We were having dinner on the first night of the trip at the Devonshire Arms Hotel in County Waterford. It's a fine hotel which belongs to an old friend of mine, Gerry Flemming, a big property and garage owner. He also promotes international variety concerts for charity, which I sometimes compère for him. As I hadn't seen him for a couple of years it was also good cover to pop down and see him in Dungarvan, which is very close to Waterford City.

He greeted Judy and me personally when we arrived, and arranged to give us a little dinner party. Unfortunately, Gerry is very interested in psychic matters so I wasn't really surprised when he said over the meal, 'I know what you're here for. You're working on the Shergar story. There must be some action around here.' I hadn't said a word about Shergar so far either to him or to Judy, but Gerry is too good a mate to lie to so I just grinned and said, 'There are a few things I have to check out.'

Judy exploded. It was the first time she had heard the word Shergar mentioned and she wasn't pleased, I can tell you.

'That's great,' she said, 'I thought you came over to see me. I didn't know you were working on a story.'

I tried to laugh it off and we didn't say too much more over dinner, but later I did my best to smooth things over. If it had been another kind of story, I don't think I'd have had too much trouble, but when I started to give Judy a few details of why I needed a cover, she got very nervous. As she was going to be with me most of the time, I told her that we would be spending some of it poking around the harbour at Waterford and around the fishing ports along the coast, looking for any signs that someone might have had something to do with moving Shergar out of the country. I explained that I believed it had been done by an international gang, helped probably by the IRA. I didn't tell her too much about where I got the information from, but Judy knew already that the IRA were often active in Waterford, and she was none too cheerful at first. Nosing around an IRA stronghold isn't really the best alternative to a loving week-end with an old boyfriend, but I promised her it would be fine and, eventually, she agreed to help.

The next morning, we drove into Waterford City and got right down to it. The cover was fine up to a point, but as I really had to ask some pretty pointed questions, I couldn't get away with just a romantic stroll along the quayside with Judy. So I decided that I'd admit I was a journalist, but say I was doing some features about Waterford and play it by ear from there. I parked on the quayside, beside a little yellow hut with a tar-paper roof which said 'Harbour Master' on it. I went in and found a rather splendid looking fellow in a smart naval-type uniform – a dark coat with brass buttons – and told him I wanted to talk to someone about the handling of cargo in the port of Waterford. It was a bit lame, but the problem was that Beag hadn't given me very much to go on. I'd come to Waterford 'looking for people' but I didn't know what to expect or even really what questions I should be asking.

I wasn't too worried, though. I'm not Irish for nothing and I know how things get done in a place like Waterford. If I just followed my nose, asking innocent questions about the harbour, it wouldn't be too long before word got around that a journalist from England was poking about.

If I did my asking carefully, I could probably drop a few hints about Shergar in due course, when the moment seemed right, and as long as I made sure everyone knew I was Irish myself – a journalist *from* Britain, but not a *British* journalist – then if someone had something to say, I knew they'd probably sidle up to me in a pub, or a café somewhere, as the trip went along.

The Harbour Master was civil enough and he suggested I see the Waterford Harbour Commissioners. He gave me a name, Mr John Boylan, and Judy and I walked over to the Commissioners' office in a big building just off the quay.

I found Boylan easily, and told him I'd like to do a formal interview about the workings of the port. He agreed, but said it would be better if the Chairman of the Harbour Commissioners, Michael McQuillan, was in on it. He introduced me, and we agreed to do the interview at the office after lunch.

I went back to the car and said to Judy: 'We've got a few hours before I see the commissioners, it's time for a quick recce.'

'And what does that mean?' she asked nervously. 'What are we going to do?'

I think the visits to the Harbour Master and the Harbour Commissioners had reassured her that it was all going to be fairly straightforward, but when I told her I wanted to start asking questions around the hotels in the port, she got very anxious again.

'Don't worry,' I said. 'Just follow me. I'll do the talking. Just be friendly. You don't have to do anything. You'll help put people at their ease just by being there.'

There are about four hotels along the waterfront and I decided to start at the far end, with the Granville Arms. I took Judy's hand and we walked up to the reception desk, bold as brass, and I started to spin the receptionist a yarn.

'I'm sorry to trouble you,' I said. 'I have a sixty-four dollar question to ask you. The only trouble is that if you answer the question correctly, I can't give you the sixty-four dollars because I'm broke.'

The girl behind the counter grinned and I knew I'd made a good start. A little joke is always the best way to kick off in Ireland.

'Look,' I went on. 'I'm looking for a couple of people who are friends of a friend of mine. They stayed in a hotel in Waterford around the 7,8,9 and 10 February. I don't know which hotel they stayed in, but one of them left a book behind with some important notes in it, and I was wondering if this was the one.'

I heard a sort of funny intake of breath beside me, and I glanced at Judy. She was staring at me sideways in absolute amazement. She'd never heard anyone tell such a cock-and-bull story so calmly before, and she just couldn't believe it.

The girl behind the counter didn't seem bothered, though, and she got out the hotel register and we went through it, going right back to the February period when Shergar was stolen. There was nothing that looked at all suspicious. All the guests were very much what you'd have expected for the time of year: mostly sales reps and businessmen representing well-known Irish and English companies.

I'd told the receptionist that one of the names might be a foreign name – that always helps to stimulate interest in Ireland – but there were no entries at all out of the ordinary. I left the Granville disappointed, and outside I had another little tiff with Judy.

'You never told me about all this,' she said. 'What are you really looking for? Who are these people who are supposed to be friends of a friend?'

She didn't say it outright but I knew she was worried about the IRA and she didn't like what was going on one little bit.

I soothed her as best I could, but I needn't have worried. There's something fascinating about a search and, despite herself, Judy quickly got caught up in it. We tried two more hotels, the Tower and the Bridge, without success, and then at the fourth and last hotel we tried – Dooley's – we finally found something unusual. By this time, Judy appeared to have stopped worrying and was really getting into the spirit of things.

The receptionist at Dooley's was a very pleasant young woman called Caroline who seemed very ready to be helpful, but when I started to spin my yarn, I found out just how much Judy's attitude had changed. As the whole story was a load of nonsense anyway, I wasn't being too careful about the details, and this time I didn't mention any book being left behind and said I was looking for three or four people.

'Oh no,' Judy interrupted seriously, 'that's not right. It was only one or two.'

I glanced at Judy and almost burst out laughing. Half an hour

55

before she had been telling me off for making up lies; now she was behaving as though she believed the story completely and was correcting me on the details! Anyway, the hotel register for February was in a separate book and Caroline agreed to go upstairs to get it. When she came back, we started to go through the entries for the period of the Shergar kidnapping, and this time a couple of names did catch my eye.

Right on the key date there were two men registered – Mr Grey and Mr Johnston – from a company called European Electronics. The address of the company was written very indistinctly, but the town was either Greenford or Greenwich. There was something wrong with the entry – as Terry Wogan is always saying, 'I could feel it in my water'. I made notes, and thanked Caroline profusely, convinced that we finally had some kind of lead.

'I know the firm,' I said. 'That must be them. I'll try and contact them through their head office.'

'That's right,' Judy said enthusiastically, 'we'll get in touch with them through the firm.'

I was relieved that Judy seemed to have got over the nervousness and was playing a full part, and we chatted about the men for a while over a sandwich and a coffee in a snack-bar along the quay.

The entry had caught my eye originally because just recently a big arms shipment had been uncovered by the customs in France. The weapons had been packed in crates marked 'electronics components' and they were believed to be intended for the IRA. I couldn't do much checking in Waterford, but resolved to do so as soon as I returned to London.

I didn't know what to make of Waterford yet, but at least I felt we were beginning to make some progress.

After lunch, I went to interview John Boylan and Michael McQuillan at the Harbour Commissioners' Office. Even though the formal part of the inteview tended to throw a bit of cold water on my theory that Shergar had been taken out by sea, I ended up more convinced than ever that it would have been possible to smuggle a horse out through Waterford. There's an old joke in journalism: 'the report was later confirmed by a denial from the authorities in . . .'. That was how I felt about the interview with the Waterford people.

John Boylan, a very pleasant, youthful-looking man in his late thirties or early forties, certainly conveyed a feeling of knowing the harbour business, and as for Michael McQuillan, who was in his sixties, he gave the impression that he had grown up with the port and had seen it through good and bad days.

After the initial sparring, I had given up the pretence that I was interested in the general aspects of cargo handling in Waterford. I told them that there had been reports and rumours circulating in England that Shergar *might* have been taken out of Ireland by this route and asked them to comment.

'It's certainly possible,' McQuillan said, 'but it's unlikely that you would get such a horse out without it being spotted. It would have to be inspected by vets, health people, customs people. Officially, I'd say it wasn't possible.'

'Tell me, Mr McQuillan,' I said, 'if I were to ask you – as a man in shipping yourself – how *you* would get Shergar out, what would you say? Would you use a container vessel, or how would you go about it?'

After some thought McQuillan replied, 'Well, I'd probably take him out on a fishing vessel. That would seem to be the best way, probably from some small cove. You would need some tackle for lifting him onto the fishing boat, then he could be transferred to a small coaster at sea.'

I turned to John Boylan.

'Mr Boylan, you handled horses here at Waterford yourself up to a few years ago, even though you don't handle them any longer. Would you go along with Mr McQuillan? Is it possible to get a horse out illegally through the port, or the surrounding area of Waterford?'

'It would be very difficult,' Boylan said, 'but I agree it would be possible illegally. It would be especially difficult through the port of Waterford itself, because of the constant monitoring and examination of all livestock. But there are numerous small coves. They're so isolated that it would be impossible to monitor movement through all of them. I don't say it wouldn't present difficulties, but I know swimming is a favourite activity of many horses and the trainers use it for exercise. It wouldn't be too difficult to have a horse swim out, say 100 yards, to a small craft, then transfer to the carrying vessel later. That's certainly a definite possibility.'

As they were both more or less convinced that there was too much surveillance for Shergar to be taken out on a regular livestock vessel, I asked if it was possible to use any other kind of vessel operating in the port itself.

John Boylan didn't seem to fancy the idea. 'It would be very difficult to get a horse on board a vessel that wasn't equipped for carrying livestock,' he said. 'It wouldn't make much sense to have a horse worth millions of pounds in the hull of a huge vessel, which would rock and shake while it was at sea.'

However, they both had to agree with me that money can change situations – especially a lot of money.

'Oh, I'm sure anything is possible, if you spend enough money on it,' McQuillan said. 'But it would be pretty hard to keep it a secret. There just aren't that many horses moved through here nowadays. Some years ago, it was so common that another horse wouldn't have meant anything at all. Nowadays, it's such an extraordinary thing, that somebody would have noticed.' McQuillan laughed. 'You can't get away with anything in this place.'

Maybe, I thought, but I was far from convinced, and I was pretty sure McQuillan and Boylan weren't convinced either. I could understand their attitude. Their position was that while it would, in theory, be possible to take Shergar out, it wasn't likely that it could be pulled off without the horses being spotted.

It was interesting, though, that their first thought – as mine had been during my telephone conversation with James Beag – was that the easiest way would be through one of the small fishing ports or coves further up the coast.

Beag had seemed definite about Dunmore East, so that was where we went – driving down the next morning after a very pleasant evening of Irish chat and good company at the Dungarvan Arms. It was a bright, warmish spring day, ideal for strolling about, and Judy and I spent most of the day on the quay at Dunmore East, chatting to fishermen. As it was Wednesday, there were plenty of them about. Friday is still fish day in Catholic Ireland and the fishermen go out on Wednesday and come in on Thursday so that they can have their fish in the big Dublin markets by Friday. The fishermen were preparing their nets and baiting lobster pots and most of them were happy to break off for a few minutes to have a chat with strangers. Having

Shergar, ridden by Walter Swinburn, won the 1981 Epsom Derby on 3 June by the biggest margin in the history of the race (*Gerry Cranham*)

After the Derby, the Aga Khan proudly leads his horse to the Winner's Enclosure
(*S&G Press Agency Ltd*)

Shergar and Walter Swinburn going down to the start of the Derby
(*Sporting Pictures (UK) Ltd*)

On 25 July 1981, again ridden by Walter Swinburn, Shergar won the King George
and Queen Elizabeth Diamond Stakes at Ascot (*S&G Press Agency Ltd*)

Shergar and his jockey are led by Dickie McCabe to the Winner's Enclosure after the King George and Queen Elizabeth Diamond Stakes (*S&G Press Agency Ltd/J. Parker*)

In October 1981 Shergar was retired to stud at Ballymany Stud in Newbridge, Co. Kildare, where he received a civic reception. He is led by Liam Foley, head stable lad at Ballymany (*Pat Maxwell picture, Dublin*)

Shergar enjoying his retirement from racing at Ballymany (*Ed Byrne*)

Shergar is welcomed to Ballymany Stud by its owner, the Aga Khan, and his family
(*both pictures Ruth Rogers*)

Superintendent Jimmy Murphy led the investigation into the kidnapping of Shergar. Here he is seen giving a press conference at Naas police headquarters — wearing his famous trilby hat (*Irish Press*)

After the kidnap of Shergar (8 February 1983) the Garda searched all studs and farms in Ireland (above) and roadchecks were in operation on all local roads (below) (*both pictures Press Association*)

"**Bejesus Mary! Did you ever see Murphy do O'Connell Street in 35 seconds before?**"

This cartoon appeared in a London newspaper shortly after the kidnap — but, sadly, it didn't solve the mystery (*kind permission of The Standard*)

An aerial view of Ballymany Stud showing, from left to right, the Fitzgerald house, the stables, the stud offices and the stallion barn (*Irish Evening Press*)

A view of the Stud taken from the Curragh side (*Pat Maxwell picture, Dublin*)

Garda officer Kreegan checking a car at the Ballymany Stud gate
(*Irish Press, Carolyn Carr*)

'After the horse has bolted.' Garda officer Peter Murphy outside Shergar's empty box. Note the brass plate on the door giving Shergar's pedigree and racing history (*Press Association*)

Daily life had to go on at the Stud, in spite of the Garda caravan at the gates, which was set up as their communications centre (*Irish Press, Carolyn Carr*)

PLEAS

Three of the Fitzgerald children shortly after their ordeal (from left to right, Margaret, Frances and Emett) with Mrs Peter Cullen, wife of the assistant head groom at Ballymany (*Carolyn Carr*)

Stan Cosgrove, Shergar's vet, with one of Shergar's filly foals, born in the spring of 1983. She has inherited her father's white blaze (*Ruth Rogers*)

Ghislain Drion, the French manager of Ballymany Stud (*Carolyn Carr*)

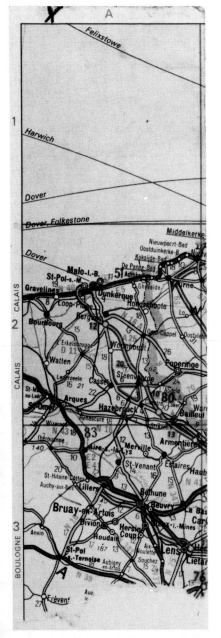

The fragment of map that was left for me at King's Cross Station. The biro mark is immediately above the word 'Bruay' in the bottom left-hand corner

The Piper Champagne Awards Luncheon

in the presence of Their Royal Highnesses, The Prince and Princess of Wales

Guest List

24th May 1983
The Dorchester Hotel
Park Lane
London

The guest list for the Piper Champagne Awards Luncheon, where Dr Kennedy's call reached me with the news of the *France Soir* story

I talked to Ghislain Drion at Sandown Park on 19 October, shortly after our second meeting. The Aga Khan and his wife are in the foreground — there to watch Nassipour and Shernazar (*Mel Fordham*)

Dr Kennedy — then the Irish Ambassador to London
(*Lafayette, Dublin*)

The late Captain Tim Rogers, one of the shareholders in the Shergar syndicate
(*Irish Press*)

Ukraine Girl and one of Shergar's filly foals at Coolmore Stud, Co. Tipperary
(*Carolyn Carr*)

Shergar's first colt foal, born 2 February 1983 out of Hilo Girl (*Press Association*)

Judy with me really helped a lot. She got a number of admiring glances and everyone was happy to talk to her – one old man even said, 'You remind me of that great film star, Elizabeth Taylor'.

There was one even older man on the quay who looked more than ready for a chat. I don't smoke, but I had some cigarettes in the car and I got them and offered them to him. I started off chatting about the fishing prospects, as I had with the other fishermen, and then I gradually turned the conversation round to pirates of the olden days around Waterford. I don't know the first thing about pirates, and I certainly don't know if Waterford ever actually had any, but I think I managed to make it sound convincing. Then, after a while, I picked my moment carefully and said, 'Someone in England even suggested that Shergar was taken out through here.'

I swear his face went white. I thought for a moment he was going to fall in the harbour. He called over a couple of other fishermen, and soon we had a small crowd.

'This man's looking for Shergar,' he said, and turned back to me. 'Tell them, what you told me.'

I said I'd been told that a horse that might have been Shergar was taken out from Dunmore East and put on a big ship. It didn't take a psychic to see that as well as the old man, two of them were really disturbed by my questions. No one would come out and say anything, but I had no doubt at all some of them were extremely uncomfortable. Eventually, I decided that I wasn't going to get anything to back up their reaction; so I asked who the best person would be to tell me if a horse could be got out of Dunmore East, even under the eyes of coastguards.

'Nicko Murphy,' the old man said. 'Try Nicko Murphy.'

They gave us directions and we went to find Murphy's house, a bungalow standing right on top of the cliff overlooking the harbour. They told me they thought Nicko must be ill as his boat was still tied up when he should have been preparing to put to sea. On the hilltop, I asked further directions at a little store beside a telephone kiosk, and eventually found the bungalow.

Nicko did have 'flu, but he still agreed to see me and we talked in the lounge of his home. He was a stocky chap, of about thirty-five, and the most striking thing about him was his eyes. They were the kind of eyes that seem to be seeing so much more than the ordinary person's; the kind that look out to sea and don't just see sea-gulls, but can read the weather and the tides.

We chatted for a bit and then I told him what my problem was. I wanted to know if the rumours I'd heard about Shergar *could* be true. Was it possible to get Shergar out in a boat around this coast?

'There's a possibility, no doubt,' Murphy said, 'but I wouldn't like to answer for what damage they might do to the horse, if the weather conditions weren't good.'

Later, Nicko was a little less emphatic. He admitted that it could be done, but only with certain kinds of boats. He reckoned you would need at least a seventy-foot boat and preferably one of the older, drifter type which had bigger hatches than most of the fishing boats currently in use. All in all, though, he felt that it was a risky business, because of the possibility of injuring the animal. He even suggested that he personally would rather take it out by plane! But when I first asked him about Shergar, he'd given me a very peculiar smile which I remembered long after the interview was over. Confirmed by a denial? It was impossible to say.

I left the bungalow and drove back down to the pier with Judy. I wanted to take a closer look at the customs arrangements since everyone seemed convinced that they had a very tight control of the situation in Waterford. When we reached the quay, the old man had gone and I drove slowly, looking for some of the people we had been talking to earlier. When we were about half way along the pier, a man ran out of the fishing sheds and said, 'You're not looking for that South African fellow, are you?'

I started to say that I wasn't, but I switched quickly and said instead, 'Yes. Do you know where he went?'

'He's gone off to see the other people.'

'You don't know where that would be, do you?'

'No. I don't know where he's gone. But I think the business is right, anyhow.'

It was a phrase I remembered very clearly when I took stock at the end of the Waterford trip. So many of the threads that I had picked up seemed to point towards arms dealing, and I began to wonder whether that might be the connection with Shergar. Had Beag mentioned Waterford not because the horse went out that way, but because arms had gone in there to pay for the kidnap – delivered to the IRA for their work on behalf of the international gang?

Yet Beag had all but said outright that the animal itself had gone out through Dunmore East. I hadn't managed to find proof, but I headed back to Dublin feeling confident that, despite everyone's reluctance to admit it, it would have been no problem at all to organize the departure of Shergar in the tight-knit little world I had just spent two days exploring.

Chapter 7

Before leaving Ireland it was time to see Detective Superintendent Jimmy Murphy – the man in charge of the official
police investigation. We'd spoken twice on the telephone the
previous week-end and I'd glimpsed him a couple of times in the
very early days of the kidnap, but I'd come far enough now to
know that I had got to meet him and – I hoped – establish a
relationship with him. I called his office, in the Naas police
headquarters, made an appointment, and drove back from
Waterford.

I had a lot to think about on the way. Superficially, it had been
a very inconclusive trip, yet I was certain I hadn't been wasting
my time. Admittedly, I was still at the stage of collecting
fragments of information, but I had the feeling that if I went on
collecting patiently, and agreed to play Beag's games, however
frustrating they were at the time, he would eventually start to fill
in some of the gaps. I couldn't rush him. Every time I'd tried to
force information out of him, he'd simply clammed up. I was
sure he could tell me the background to what I'd found out in
Waterford – every last damned detail probably, but it would be
in his own time. What I wanted to do was see whether anything I
knew fitted in with what the police had found out, and to check
that I had to start getting a bit closer to Murphy.

I had a little time to spare before my meeting with him so I
called Captain Sean Berry, the manager of the Irish Thoroughbred Breeders' Association. I wanted to see whether he would be
interested in increasing the Association's £50,000 reward offer.
He was very busy on several projects and the only time he could
see me was after I was due to sail back to Liverpool. I couldn't
put off my return to England, so very briefly, on the phone, we
discussed the possibility of raising the reward and agreed to talk

62

in more detail later.

I drove with Judy into the town of Kildare and, as I still had some time to spare, I tried to see Shergar's vet, Stan Cosgrove. I knew that he had played a big part in the events immediately after the kidnap, and I was hoping to ask his help with a number of details. When the groom, Jimmy Fitzgerald, had been picked up by his brother Des after being dropped by the kidnappers near Kilcock, they had called the stud manager, Ghislain Drion, and Drion's first call had been to Stan Cosgrove.

According to my information, Cosgrove and Drion had rushed over to Ballymany and the two of them had gone to the stallion barn to make sure that Shergar was really missing. I'd been told by a reliable source that they'd been too scared to go near the house, because they were afraid the kidnappers might still be around. I'd heard also that once the police had been told – many hours after the event – it was Cosgrove who had called Captain Berry, at 5.30 a.m., to fill him in. Later, after Cosgrove had attended mass at 7.30 on the kidnap morning, he had breakfasted with Captain Berry and gone over the events with him.

I would very much have liked to talk to Cosgrove about that morning, but after calling at his practice on the Monday, before going to Waterford, and getting the brush-off, I never held much hope of finding him.

At the yard this time, I identified myself to a woman in the office yet again, and said I'd like to see Mr Cosgrove. She took my card and disappeared up a spiral staircase at the back of the office. Ten minutes later she came back. Mr Cosgrove was too busy. He couldn't see me. It was obvious that 'couldn't' meant 'wouldn't'. I was disappointed and I was also surprised. I knew Cosgrove had been talking to some of the local Irish press and yet he was refusing even to *see* me, although I'd made a big point of letting him know that I was Irish. If I had been a British journalist, I could have understood his refusal. British journalists had a really bad reputation in the area. Right from the beginning of the Shergar story, they had upset the locals. After six or seven days, once the trail was cold, they had become very frustrated and had turned the whole affair into a circus, harassing people around the village and the Stud and inventing stories. The local Irish had just clammed up – except when they wanted to make a few pounds telling some wild fantasies to the clowns of Fleet Street!

I knew from close friends in the business that the editor of one British national newspaper had become so angry at paying out expenses to his reporters without getting a decent story in return that he had told them to find a dead horse and manufacture a story.

'Just find a dead horse,' he'd yell at them, 'any old horse. Photograph it, and we'll pretend it's Shergar. At least we'll have a story for one day!'

Anyway, I could see I wasn't going to persuade Stan Cosgrove to change his mind, so I went to see Kiernan Breedan instead. He hadn't been Shergar's vet, but he was one of the most respected vets in the Curragh and he knew the local scene intimately.

We talked about the air of depression that had been cast over the whole bloodstock industry by the Shergar kidnapping.

'When a stallion worth millions of pounds is kidnapped and there's no trace of him for several weeks, we shudder to think of what other possibilities there are,' he said.

He told me he'd thought at first that the whole kidnap story had been a joke. He simply hadn't believed such a thing could happen. It was, as he put it, 'undreamed of in Ireland'.

I asked him what condition he thought Shergar might be in, if he was still alive, and his reply was cautious.

'There must have been a horse man on the kidnap team to handle him and load him and things like that,' Breedan said, 'but Shergar wasn't a difficult stallion. He hadn't a reputation for an awkward temperament or anything like that. They're probably keeping him on a minimum diet, so he won't get too fresh and start playing up. If there is a horse man on the team, he won't be filling Shergar with oats, filling him with energy. If he was kept on maximum feeding, then they'd have to exercise him, and there'd be too much chance of him being seen. I'd say they'd have him stabled on a minimum maintenance diet.'

Breedan was concerned, however, that they might be using tranquilizers

'If they used tranquilizers constantly this would have the side effect of causing protrusion of the penis, which leads to ulceration and soreness and the inability to retract it. That could

64

definitely do permanent harm, especially to a stallion at stud.'

Finally, I asked Breedan what he though about getting Shergar out of Ireland.

He shared the view that it would be extremely difficult for the kidnappers to use official routes. He pointed out that because of fears of animals importing disease, most countries placed far more restrictions on horses than they did on people.

'In fact,' he said, 'as travel for human beings is loosening up, passport and medical document control for animals is being tightened.'

The whole interview produced the kind of common sense I would have expected from a vet as experienced as Kiernan Breedan. But, alas, he had no inside information. For that, I would have to turn to Superintendent Murphy, but I also knew that it would take time. I couldn't just rush in and expect Murphy to take me into his confidence. Nor could I be completely frank about James Beag at that stage, though I could describe the calls in some detail.

In the months that followed, I became good friends with Murphy. We developed a relationship of mutual liking and trust, and when I look back at the first interview I had with him, I have to smile. He gave me very much the 'official view' of events; he was very friendly and courteous, particularly once he knew something of my background, but our deeper exchanges would only come later.

Leaving Judy outside in the car, I interviewed him at the Naas police headquarters, which are right in the middle of Naas Town. The police station is next to the court-house and a little way down from Naas's famous hotel and restaurant, the Lawlors Hotel. It's an old building, and you go in through an impressive little courtyard. Superintendent Murphy's office is up two flights of stairs, a small room, very much like policemen's offices the world over, crowded with maps, papers and filing cabinets.

Murphy is in his late fifties, a shortish man of about five feet eight inches. The best way to picture him is as a father figure, and he's regarded as such by the whole district; the kind of favourite father any boy would be proud to introduce to his schoolfriends. He has a strong country accent and he's a very gentle sort of man, well-mannered, easy to get along with. But he's also nobody's fool. He's had a lot of successes as a police officer, and he is very well respected in the local community.

One of his most successful cases happened shortly after he moved from Waterford to Kildare. Jimmy 'Jazzer' Murphy, as he was called, was confronted with one of the biggest art robberies in Europe. Thieves broke into the home of Sir Alfred Beit, at Russborough in County Wicklow, and stole some of the most valuable paintings in the world. The whole break-in had the hallmark of experts, but Jimmy Murphy, after a painstaking investigation, arrested Dr Rose Dugdale, an English lady who was living in Ireland and who became involved in the early struggles and problems of Northern Ireland. She was eventually charged and found guilty and sent to prison at Limerick.

That wasn't how the British press had chosen to portray him, though. When the Shergar story started to slow down, Fleet Street had been casting around desperately for something to liven it up and, sadly, they'd picked on Jimmy Murphy. They'd portrayed him as a bumbling country cop – a kind of Irish Inspector Clouseau. He usually wears a battered trilby hat and some of the journalists had gone down to the local store and bought hats like his. When he appeared on the steps of the police station to give a press conference, wearing his trilby, there they all were in their Murphy hats, ready for the photographers. It was an easy, cheap-running gag: the dumb Irish village inspector, getting nowhere because he was out of his depth.

As an Irishman who knows Irish country life and politics intimately, I had a much sharper picture of Murphy. I knew he was a good policeman, but I could also recognize a good scapegoat when I saw one – and I don't just mean a scapegoat for the British press. Other people needed scapegoats too, and Murphy was a perfect candidate. I was convinced even at the time of our first meeting – and I now know it for certain – that Murphy was given very limited information; it was a classic case of being told too little too late. He had only limited co-operation both from his own Irish authorities, and from Ballymany Stud. His hands were partially tied most of the time, and I felt really angry about his position.

I felt quite funny going to see him for the first time. It's always an odd feeling for a village boy, or a city boy like myself, to talk to an Irish cop. I've dealt with all kinds of policemen – in the

United States, in Britain, in Spain – but on your own home ground it's different. When you've been brought up in a village in Ireland, you know that the first person you turn to is the priest, the second is the policeman. And they in turn know everything that's going on. When I went up the stairs to see him, I couldn't help feeling a bit like a kid again, but Murphy very soon put me at ease.

Our first meeting was much more formal than later ones. It wasn't formal in the sense of being staid: we had a few good jokes and a chat, but we were both getting the measure of each other and I was content to lay a foundation to our relationship which could be developed later.

Despite the formality, and a little bit of fencing on both sides, Murphy *did* go straight to the heart of one really crucial point in the investigation. The fact that it had been hobbled from the start because of Ballymany's lack of communication. The crux of Jimmy Murphy's problem was that the horse had been kidnapped between half past eight and nine o'clock on the night of 8 February, and he had only been informed officially at five minutes to five on the following morning.

As Murphy himself said ruefully, 'The delay gave them plenty of time to take the horse to any part of Ireland – and out of the country, too, if they had laid on special transportation, such as a plane.'

At this first interview, Murphy explained the delay in starting the investigation.

'Well, it appears that Mr Fitzgerald was threatened by the kidnappers. He was told not to say anything about it, and specifically not to tell the Garda about it. He did not come back to Ballymany Stud until some time around 1.00 a.m. He then informed the manager of the Stud, who had to ensure that the animal had in fact been taken, and Mr Drion did say to me that it was difficult for them to accept the story for a while, and that he had to check it out for himself. That was mostly the cause of the delay.'

I knew already that this 'cause' was linked to several other 'causes' – the principal one being that Ghislain Drion had not had enough confidence to make even the simplest move without consulting his boss, the Aga Khan. I'd heard about Drion and Cosgrove being afraid to go into the barn and the house but why,

I wondered, if they believed the kidnappers were still there, hadn't they called the police straightaway? I was to find out more about this problem, and its implications, in the weeks to come, but it was obvious already that Murphy had been given an impossible handicap right from the off.

In the two months since the kidnap, Murphy had had the hardest task ever set a policeman in Ireland. While we were getting to know each other, he described to me what it had been like from the early stages of the investigation.

'The first few days were very hectic,' he said. 'Many people were ringing up. All the Irish people were disturbed and depressed over the animal having been taken and indeed they offered many suggestions. We were going practically day and night for the first two weeks and then things began to rain off, though we still pursued our inquiries and we are still pursuing them. We have searched and researched the whole of Ireland. The RUC [the Royal Ulster Constabulary] assisted us. All the farmers have been invited and requested by their own organization to search farms and to search adjoining farms, on two different occasions, and we ourselves have carried out various searches thoughout the country. We also had two general searches and we still came up with nothing.'

His overall conclusion was devastating.

'Unfortunately, nothing of value has been passed on to us, and while many people have contacted us by telephone, and written to us, and we have probed all that information, *we are still more or less as we were on the night the animal was taken.*' (My italics).

Cautiously, I brought the subject round to rewards and ransoms. I knew I had to move carefully, because whatever Jimmy Murphy's private views might be, the police were officially committed to oppose all ransom payments and all payments which might be construed as ransom.

Murphy dealt first with the ransom demand made in the early days of the kidnap.

'Jimmy Fitzgerald was told on the night of the kidnap that a ransom would be sought on the following day, and was told to convey this to his manager or the manager of the Stud. The ransom demand was in fact made on the Wednesday following the taking. There were two calls in all. One was a preliminary call because the manager of the Stud wasn't there, and the second call was the demand for a ransom of two million pounds.'

I asked what Ghislain Drion's reaction had been.

'Well, he's only the manager, of course. He would have no negotiating powers at all and he would have to contact the syndicate to know what they were prepared to do.'

As I anticipated, there was no doubt about Murphy's position on the issue.

'I would not favour the payment of a ransom in any circumstances, and I've made that quite clear from the beginning,' he said.

So at that stage his views on the payment of a reward weren't too encouraging for James Beag.

I asked him if he didn't think that the £10,000 offered by *The Sporting Life* and the £50,000 offered by the Irish Thoroughbred Breeders' Association were ridiculously small amounts to offer for a horse worth at least ten million pounds.

'I could accept that point,' he said, 'but on the other hand, if the reward is made any higher, you are going into the field of ransom and then I would have to take another view. I don't mind the reward being paid, but I would assume that the reward would go to a person who had nothing to do with the taking and that is why I would like to see it kept reasonably low. If it goes up to half a million or a million pounds, then you're going into the ransom field, and this I would oppose.'

I knew that the point Murphy was making would come up again and again as I tried to raise the reward for Beag. Is a reward paid to a member of the gang – if indeed Beag was a member of the gang – ransom under another name? I didn't necessarily believe so. Even if Beag had been involved, if he were prepared to sell out his colleagues and allow the horse to be recovered – even if he didn't actually turn 'Queen's evidence' – then I felt that that was better than allowing Shergar to be ill-treated or killed. I'd had the feeling for a while now that not enough people involved in the affair really cared about the horse. To me, a horse is much more than an investment or a property; it is a living creature, to be loved and respected, and you can't just write it off and make an insurance claim, as you do with a car or a broken roof.

In that, at least, I had a kindred spirit in Jimmy Murphy.

'Oh yes, I love horses,' he said, when I put the question to him. 'I love horses and in my single days I travelled to many race meetings throughout the country and in England. I love racing, I love horses and I don't believe that any Irishman, or anyone who has a drop of Irish blood in him and who's seen anything of horses and horse-racing, could destroy a fine animal. I don't believe it could happen.'

They were sentiments I could only agree with, but I was less convinced than Murphy was that we were talking about Irish kidnappers. In that early interview, he was very sceptical about the possibility that it had been an international gang. He agreed that an international terrorist organization could have been involved, but he was convinced that they would have had to act through an Irish group, with local knowledge.

Interestingly, when I asked him about the possible role of Ireland's illegal organizations, and after two months' investigation, he said quite categorically, 'Nothing has led me to believe that the IRA or the INLA [the Irish National Liberation Army] were involved.'

At the end of my talk with Murphy I felt I had made a good start in winning his trust. In between the formal inquiries, he had quizzed me quite a lot about my background and attitudes and I felt that I had managed to put myself in a quite different category from the wild men of Fleet Street who had been plaguing him since the investigation began. But I was still a long way from getting Shergar back. Beag was taking his time in coming 'up front', as the Americans say, and until he did, the people I was talking to in Ireland weren't likely to be tempted away from their existing attitudes. At that stage, I could only hope that the next phone calls from Beag would start to quicken the pace.

Chapter 8

When I got back to England, after saying goodbye to Judy in Dublin, I decided that I had better start being a bit bolder in pressing James Beag's demands for a bigger reward. I had no particular liking for Beag, since it was obvious that even if he wasn't a fully-fledged gang member, he was certainly connected with the kidnapping in some way. On the other hand, I had a great love for Shergar and I didn't want to see the animal slaughtered while people argued over the technical differences between ransoms and rewards.

On reflection, I'd come to think of Beag as a fringe member of the gang; close enough to know what was going on, but not close enough to get a share of the confidence money I was convinced had been paid. I decided that the best way to project him was as a 'weak link' in the gang, someone who could be turned by money just as a member of a terrorist gang or a team of armed robbers can be turned into a 'supergrass' by the offer of immunity and a new life.

Fortunately, just as I was deciding to try to hot up my efforts to obtain a bigger reward, I found a good ally in one of the syndicate members, Captain Tim Rogers. We'd talked briefly a couple of times about the kidnapping, but I decided to make a more frank approach to him, and discovered that he took a far less rigid view of rewards and ransoms than Superintendent Jimmy Murphy did.

Captain Rogers was a fine gentleman, with an outstanding reputation in the Irish horse world as a breeder and owner of one of the best studs in Ireland. Very sadly, he died on New Year's Day, 1984. He was also one of the shareholders in Shergar. He made it very clear that he was totally opposed to paying ransom, but, like me, he did not feel that a sum of around

71

£100,000 or £150,000 would automatically be too high to be considered a reward.

He also believed strongly that it was up to the owning syndicate to put up a reward, rather than leaving the initiative to the Irish Thoroughbred Breeders' Association or a sporting newspaper. He told me that he personally would be willing to put up a share of a reward. He pointed out that there were thirty-four shareholders in all. He would be happy to go up to £5,000 himself, an example which could bring the total for the syndicate up to a maximum of £200,000, if they all followed suit.

It was during the course of my conversation with Captain Rogers that I got confirmation of the strains that existed between certain syndicate members and the special committee, chaired by Drion, set up by the Aga Khan to handle the Shergar affair – supposedly on behalf of the whole syndicate. Captain Rogers was very reluctant to talk to me at first, and he hinted that he had been specifically asked not to. He was too much of a gentleman to say so, but I happened to know already that a telex message had been sent from Ballymany to members of the syndicate, and so presumably to Captain Rogers, urging them to be as secretive as possible. I'd been told that the telex said in part:

> the committee stresses in the strongest possible terms the continued requirement for security and urges all shareholders to comply. Public speculation and individual initiative can only jeopardize this delicate case and are against the interests of the syndicate. The committee regrets that some shareholders have not complied with this request in the past and urges everyone to do so in the future.

Luckily for me, and unluckily for the management at Ballymany, a number of members of the syndicate didn't agree that secrecy was essential. Several members felt that it was all very well to try to stifle 'public speculation and individual initiative' as long as the syndicate committee was showing plenty of initiative of its own, and that didn't appear to them to be the case. In fact, the shareholders who were criticized in the telex for not having complied with earlier requests for secrecy had not done so just to be bloody-minded, but because they believed the committee was using a cloak of secrecy to cover up its own shortcomings and lack of decisive action. Among the share-holders were some very powerful individuals, men who were as knowledgeable as any in the horse world. They might not be as rich as the Aga Khan and they might not own as much of Shergar as he did, but they were far too experienced to sit by meekly at the behest of the Ballymany Stud when they felt they were not getting enough action to protect their investment in Shergar.

I asked Captain Rogers about the reports I was hearing of dissatisfaction within the syndicate about the handling of the affair. His answer was cautious, but its meaning unmistakable.

'I've been in the business a long time,' he told me, 'and I think I can say I know it backwards. I don't want to say anything that would jeopardize what's happening at the moment, but I would probably not have handled it in this manner. That's all I'm prepared to say and leave it at that.'

I pressed him a little and asked whether he was worried about the handling by the syndicate or by the police.

'I'm not talking about the police,' Captain Rogers said. 'They've got their own methods. I'm talking about the basic handling of the syndicate committee.'

Finally, I asked him specifically about the way the syndicate seemed to be failing to agree on some kind of initiative to put up a reward. In the process, I painted a rather fanciful picture of James Beag, but it was along these lines that I was coming to picture him.

'Captain Rogers,' I said. 'Would you agree with me that there could be a weak link out there? Someone who had to reconnoitre the place for the kidnappers perhaps? Someone who had to check to see if Shergar was at Ballymany? He'd only have been paid £1,000 or £2,000 by the gang that took the horse. That £1,000 or £2,000 is probably gone by now, because the man went to Cheltenham or to Aintree to the Grand National, or maybe he's been to the first meeting at Phoenix Park and blown his money. Now, if there was a bigger reward it might entice him out of the wood. Would you not see the thing like that?'

Captain Rogers wouldn't commit himself, but the criticism of Ballymany implied in his answer was clear enough.

'All I'm empowered to say,' Captain Rogers said, 'is that I would not have handled the thing the way it has been handled.'

Acquiring such a respected ally as Captain Rogers was a very encouraging development, but I knew that it would be far from easy to get the rest of the syndicate to follow suit and, spurred on by the fact that Captain Rogers had not set his face against the idea of a bigger reward, I decided to press Beag's 'demand' in even higher quarters.

I'd already arranged to see the Irish Ambassador in London at the time, Dr Eamonn Kennedy. An appointment was set for Sunday, 17 April, and I decided that at the meeting I would go all out to try to persuade him to ask the Irish Government to help with a reward.

The meeting took place at the Irish Embassy in Grosvenor Place and, as I might have expected, it was one of the most agreeable interludes in the whole search for Shergar. Dr Kennedy is, in the true sense of the word, a diplomat: highly regarded at the Court of St James and by fellow members of the diplomatic corps, he had also made a strong and favourable impression on the Irish community he was representing in London. He is in his early fifties and has a stocky, well-designed physique. His light brown hair and fine moustache all help the diplomatic image. He had just driven up from spending Sunday with friends in the country and we talked for two and a half hours in his private quarters over snacks and drinks provided by Mrs Kennedy.

Fortunately, I had met the Kennedys on several occasions and we had become friends. Dr Kennedy was also familiar with my broadcasting and my work in the racing world, which made the conversation very much easier. I began by giving him a complete and very frank run-down on the Shergar situation, as I saw it at that time. I told him the whole story of the Shergar kidnapping, including many details that he was not aware of – in particular the reasons for the stud's long delay in informing the police. I told him about my interviews with Lord Derby and Jonathan Irwin and my other contacts with interested people, and, for the first time, I was completely frank to a third party about my conversations with James Beag. Dr Kennedy was fascinated by the mystery phone calls. He immediately christened him 'deep throat' and asked for every detail I could remember. I also told him about my infuriating trip to Jury's hotel and my recent trip to Waterford.

74

I told him that I believed that there was a chance of getting Shergar back alive, provided someone was prepared to improve on the offer of £60,000 in reward money that was presently available. I told him that I thought some new initiative was necessary because the situation seemed to have reached a deadlock, mainly because of inertia and inefficiency on all sides. I told him, in my opinion, that Superintendent Murphy – whom I called both before and after my visit to Dr Kennedy to keep him posted – was working with his hands tied, running an investigation with inadequate resources and inadequate co-operation from the Ballymany Stud. We discussed Ghislain Drion and his apparent unwillingness to talk to people. I put my feelings on this point very strongly, saying that it seemed to me absurd that Drion should be sending out telex messages to syndicate members ordering them, in effect, to leave everything to him, while at the same time apparently doing very little.

We also talked about the implications of the kidnapping for the whole bloodstock breeding industry in Ireland – an industry that is worth around one-hundred million pounds a year to the country. Dr Kennedy didn't need to be told what the consequences could be if the kidnapping, or indeed the poor handling of the investigation, scared off investors or encouraged those foreigners already breeding horses in Ireland to pull out.

After a long and carefully argued preamble, I put my two specific requests to Dr Kennedy. I asked if there was any way he could arrange, through diplomatic channels, for me to see the Aga Khan or, failing that, whether he could use his diplomatic and government contacts to get me in to see Ghislain Drion at Ballymany. He said he would see what he could do, though he made it clear that my request was not an easy one. I grinned, acknowledging that, and I warned that my second request would be even more difficult. I wanted to ask his help in trying to persuade the Irish Government to increase the reward money.

Immediately we came up against the old problem of rewards and ransoms. Dr Kennedy felt that any large sum might be construed as being a form of ransom, and if the Government *did* intervene, the payment would have to be handled with extreme caution. For the Government to be accused of paying ransom would be bad enough, Dr Kennedy said, but there was still the widespread feeling that the IRA or the INLA were somehow involved, and it was unthinkable for the Irish Government to be put in a position where it could be accused of paying off illegal organizations.

After careful discussion, however, Dr Kennedy accepted my view that it was possible for a sum of around £100,000 or £150,000 to be handled as a genuine reward, and he asked me which Irish Government department would be the most likely to help.

I said he could try acting through the Department of Agriculture and Fisheries, and that he could also go through the Ministry of Finance, which controls the purse strings of Bord na gCapall, the Irish Horse Board.

I mentioned also that I had considered making an approach through the former Taoiseach (Irish Prime Minister), Mr Charles Haughey, the leader of the Fianna Fail party. Haughey was himself a horse owner and breeder and I thought his intervention could be useful. One of Dr Kennedy's strengths as an ambassador is that he is on good terms with peoples of all political colourings in Ireland, and I knew he would be able to talk to Charles Haughey as easily as to Garret FitzGerald, the Prime Minister of the day.

In summing up, Dr Kennedy was extremely cautious. His personal view, he said, was that a bigger reward could be useful in the circumstances, provided it was handled with the greatest delicacy. He left me in no doubt, however, that he did not believe I had passed him over an easy task.

'I'll have to go through channels, and they may be very complicated channels,' he said. 'Don't expect miracles from me.'

I certainly didn't expect miracles, but I was delighted that the meeting had gone as well as it had. I had enormous personal respect for Dr Kennedy and I was very glad to have his sympathetic ear. I admit, too, that I was relieved to have told someone in authority the whole story of my contacts with James Beag. I trusted Dr Kennedy and he was the ideal person to 'come clean' with. I had no idea where my dealings with Beag were leading, and I was very pleased to have everything 'on record' with the Ambassador, in case it all started to go haywire. Also, because of the easy relations which already existed between us, I was able to be slightly less formal and I managed to convey to the Ambassador how strongly my love of horses was pushing me on in the search. I told him that I had a terrible image in my mind sometimes of Shergar tied up in a berth somewhere, choking himself on a rope for lack of space and care, and I urged him to try and not let too much more time be wasted in the progress through 'channels'.

He promised he would do his best, and I left the meeting feeling that I had a real ally, even though he could not be a miracle-worker.

That night, I called Captain Sean Berry and told him about my conversation with Dr Kennedy. At the same time I hinted about the information I was getting from Beag, without going into the details of how it was coming. Captain Berry was all in favour of Dr Kennedy's proposed intervention, though he joked that Bord na gCapall, the Horse Board, wasn't a very likely source of money as, as far as he knew, it was pretty well broke!

The chat to Captain Berry took an interesting turn, however, when we were discussig how the reward money should be handled, assuming that the Government or some other body could be found to put it up. Captain Berry insisted that, whatever else happened, Ballymany shouldn't be allowed to handle it, and he left me in no doubt that he didn't have a very high opinion of Ghislain Drion and his associates at the Stud. I told him that a number of syndicate members weren't happy with the situation at Ballymany either and Captain Berry admitted that he wasn't surprised. He said that he had had great difficulty communicating with the Stud on more than one occasion. His exact phrase, I recall, was that he had met with 'absolute stonewall tactics'.

It was useful to have further confirmation of what were beginning to look like serious misgivings about Ballymany among those close to the situation, and I promised to keep in touch with Captain Berry if Dr Kennedy's moves bore fruit.

I then called Captain Rogers to brief him on the meeting with Dr Kennedy and he, too, was pleased that something might be underway. All in all, I was satisfied with the latest developments, but I knew that what was needed now was a significant move from James Beag.

Chapter 9

Beag's next call lasted barely thirty seconds and strangely, for him, he made it to the LBC studios. My colleagues at LBC knew, vaguely, that I was in contact with someone who was providing information on the Shergar story. They had been warned not to press for details if a 'mystery caller' came on the line, but inevitably people *do* say 'who shall I say is calling?' when someone asks for Colin Turner. On this occasion Beag asked for me and was asked to give a name. He simply made one up – I have forgotten now what it was – and was put through to my extension in the news-room.

'What's happening?' Beag asked.

I told him that when I'd been in Ireland I'd seen a lot of people. 'I still don't know why the hell I went to Waterford,' I said.

'Did it go well?'

He didn't sound very interested.

I said I'd seen one or two strange things, including the names of two suspicious men, which I hadn't had time to check out yet.

This was true, I'd been very busy since my return and I hadn't had a chance to check properly on European Electronics, though I had looked through all the postal and commercial directories, as well as asking British Telecom information, and discovered that there was no such company as European Electronics in either Greenford or Greenwich! Nor had I been able to follow through on my instincts about livestock shipping out of the port. When I got back to England, I had started doing some serious homework about the shipping of livestock out of Waterford. I found out the Boylan and McQuillan had been telling me the truth – the export in horses was on the decline – but that was not the whole story. Though the actual number of animals shipped was falling, non-thoroughbred horses were being exported regularly to all the European Community countries and to the Middle East. What was more, the trade was being carried out in a more and more sophisticated way, using containers, rather than the old-fashioned livestock vessels. Containers passed through Waterford on their way to European ports, and to Iran, Egypt, Kuwait and Libya, carrying – according to official Irish Government information – non-throughbred horses, who were often loaded into the containers at the farm of origin.

Whatever the Waterford Harbour Commissioners' official view was, it didn't take a tremendous stretch of the imagination to see Shergar, his white socks suitably disguised with dye, slipped into a container at night on a farm, miles away from Waterford, along with some ordinary animals. All that would be needed then would be to pay the right man at the right time to look the other way when a routine consignment of non-thoroughbred horses was passing through.

After my trip to Waterford, nothing would convince me that that was impossible.

'I didn't find what I was looking for,' I said, making it obvious I meant Shergar.

I could tell from his response that he definitely wasn't interested in talking about Waterford, and his next question made it clear why.

'Is there any news yet?' he said.

He had a special way of saying 'news' which meant 'was there any news about money'.

I repeated that I'd been in touch with a number of people but nothing had actually come through.

'So there's no news [money] yet?'

'No,' I said, 'nothing's going to happen for a while yet. People are going to see what's available.'

'When will you know?'

I said, 'Leave me alone for a while. It's bound to take a bit of time.'

Beag started to ask me something else, but there was an interruption. News-rooms are very open noisy places and someone walked up to the LBC motoring correspondent, who was standing close to me, and started talking to him.

When Beag heard them, he said, 'What's that? What's that?' in a panicky voice.

I started to explain, but it was no good. The line was already dead.

The week continued normally. I went to Cheltenham on Wednesday, 20 April for the Courage International Challenge between British and Irish jockeys and, between times, I made a few phone calls to keep everyone up-to-date with the situation following my meeting with the Irish Ambassador. I'd called the Embassy and been told that the talk with Dr Kennedy had resulted in a meeting within the Department of Agriculture and Finance in Dublin. It sounded promising but the Embassy had not yet received a full report of the outcome.

When I talked to Captain Berry he confirmed that something appeared to be moving.

'I just got a kind of wrinkle that there might be something coming, but it was indirect and I don't know how true it was,' he said.

Captain Berry also said he had talked to Jonathan Irwin and learned that there was some gossip about the possibility that the Irish Thoroughbred Breeders' Association might be given clearance to raise its reward higher than £50,000. I said I'd try to contact Irwin but Captain Berry reminded me that he was off to Kentucky because Goff's were opening a subsidiary there.

I talked to Captain Rogers again and learned that he was due to have a meeting with Ghislain Drion at Ballymany. I also discovered that the Aga Khan had just formally filed his insurance claim. He was claiming for his own shares and for those shares which were being bought from him by instalments. Apparently several shareholders had not paid him for the £250,000 share all in one lump sum, and the Aga Khan had taken out policies on their shares, leaving the buyers to pay the insurance premiums, in addition to the instalments they owed him.

I called Superintendent Murphy and told him to keep his eye open for developments within the Government as there seemed to be a possibility that the reward might be increased, and then spent much of the rest of the week wondering whether I had scared Beag off for good.

I needn't have worried. He waited until the following Thursday – 28 April – and then called, as he often did, at a really inconvenient time.

I was due to have a very important lunch at noon that day at the Inn on the Park, in Park Lane. I had to discuss a project with some business colleagues, which would involve me in presenting virtually all of the top classic horse-races in Britain, Ireland and France in the coming year for video, and my thoughts were very much on preparing for the meeting. Beag called just before 9.00 a.m., using the code which meant he wanted me to go to King's Cross.

Cursing small-sized mystery men in no uncertain terms, I put on slacks and shirt and raced to King's Cross. I arrived well within the half-hour allotted under our system, but even though the call-box was free, no call came. After the breaking-off of the last call, I didn't want to miss a chance to talk to him and I waited and waited, wishing I had taken the time to put on a suit so that I could have gone straight on to the Inn on the Park if necessary.

More than an hour passed and still there was no call. It was the first time he had ever failed to make contact after using the code system and I began to get very edgy as I wondered why. Looking back on it now, after many months, it's hard to reconstruct my fears at that time, but I always had the feeling that I was being swept along in a situation that could have all kinds of disastrous implications, and of which I could see only the surface.

Even though I had done nothing illegal, I was involved with people who almost certainly had. I didn't actually believe the Shergar kidnapping was a normal IRA job, but it seemed likely that they had had a hand in it somewhere. That meant the Security Services would be following the case, as well as the police, and I could well be marked down as an associate of terrorists.

Nor did I know what was going on within the gang itself. If Beag was preparing to sell them out, as now seemed likely, they might easily find out and decide to dispose of him. What if the next step was to decide that Colin Turner, as Beag's accomplice, should go the same way?

As I stood at King's Cross I wondered if Beag was watching me, waiting for me to move so he could follow me. Had he summoned me to King's Cross to get me out of my flat? Or was someone else playing games with me? Other members of the gang? The police? The Security Services?

Eventually I decided to leave. I had to get back to change for the video lunch – it was too important a business meeting to miss, even for Beag – but I left the station with a real sense of impending disaster.

I went to the car park with all kinds of thoughts racing through my head: I imagined people following me; I saw myself being watched through binoculars; I had a vision of my flat being turned upside down while I was waiting at the station. My car was a red Renault Fuego. Nice and conspicuous, I thought. Easy to spot and easy to follow.

As I jumped into my car, I admit I was in a bit of a panic. I'd had too much time to think while hanging around at the station. I just wanted to get the hell out of there as quickly as possible. I turned on the ignition and put the car into reverse, even before I had fastened my seat-belt or looked in the rear-view mirror. Then, as I started to pull out, I looked through the offside wing-mirror and saw that it was partly obscured by a twist of paper, stuck down the side of the chrome housing.

There are sometimes a few kids playing in the car park at King's Cross and I thought someone had been fooling around. I glanced at the side of the car and at the bonnet. There were no signs of damage or vandalism, so I wound down the window to pull the paper out, and dropped it on the ground. I fastened my seat-belt and started to make my way out of the station car park. Fortunately, as it turned out, I was held up by a woman driving a yellow Mini. She was having difficulty in parking, making several runs at backing into a tight parking space, and the delay gave me time to collect my thoughts a bit.

It hit me suddenly that I'd probably done an incredibly stupid thing, and thrown away a piece of paper that could have some connection with Beag. I managed to squeeze past the Mini driver and did a right turn to swing back round the car park. The space I had left was still empty and the piece of paper was still there where I had dropped it. It was only a tiny piece, even before I had partially screwed it up. I got out of the car, picked it up and, without looking at it, got back in and set off like a Formula One driver.

I just couldn't get out of King's Cross fast enough! If the paper meant anything, it meant I *was* being watched. Someone knew my car and had either trailed me from my flat or picked me up when I arrived at King's Cross to respond to Beag's signal. I didn't know which I was most scared of – a trap by the gang or some trick by the police. I put my foot down hard and swerved out of the car park. Once on the main road I tried as best I could to see whether I was being followed, and it was only when I'd driven for more than a mile and hadn't spotted anyone taking an obvious interest in me that I took time, while waiting at a traffic light, to glance at the piece of paper.

I expected it to be a message of some kind, a note or a suggestion for a new code system, perhaps. I flattened out the paper on the passenger seat beside me, and saw that it was a fragment of a map. It wasn't a photostat, but a piece of a real map, less than six inches long and not much more than an inch and a half wide. I didn't recognize the area but I saw straight-away from the names that it was a map of a part of France. I was too nervous to take time to study it then and I took my first good look at it when I was back in my flat – which, mercifully, had not been vandalized, searched or blown up!

I was running so late for the video lunch that I examined the map while pulling on my suit and generally tidying myself up. It was, as I'd first thought, somewhere in France, but closer inspection showed that it was in fact part of the border between France and Belgium, right on the Channel coast, almost directly facing Dover, in the area known as the Pas de Calais.

The best-known place on it was the French port of Dunkirk. There were no other big towns and most of the other places would be better known to veterans of the two world wars who had fought through this area. I did find one biro mark on the map, but there were no clues as to what it meant. Oh Jaysus, I thought, another mystery. Always hints, and teasing half clues, never anything solid.

I got to the lunch and I really wasn't at my best. Instead of giving my full attention to the details of the video project, I spent half the time staring out of the restaurant window and wondering what the map could mean. One of the guests who knew me well asked what was wrong. He said he'd never seen me looking so worried. I covered up as best I could, got through the lunch, and went back to the LBC studios.

I decided that until I'd had a bit of time to digest the new situation, I would do nothing about the map. I wouldn't mention it to Superintendent Murphy or any other contacts before I'd begun to have some idea of what it might mean. There were several obvious possibilities.

The first was that the map showed where Shergar was hidden, but that didn't seem very likely. Beag was in the process of trying to raise £100,000 or £150,000 for that information; he was hardly likely to stick it in my wing-mirror for free.

Alternatively, it could be a place which the horse had passed through. The map included a big port, Dunkirk, the Franco-Belgian border and a number of much smaller ports and fishing villages. The landscape itself, as far as I could recall, was flat and pretty featureless. I didn't have the first idea what I was looking for! The biro mark could be significant, but it wasn't on a village or a town and, anyway, to be frank, I didn't feel in the mood to go probing possible terrorist hide-outs on my own.

The only other connection with France so far – apart from the fact that it was Ghislain Drion's homeland – was Beag's claim that the 'confidence money' on Flight 208 had been paid in Paris. Was the actual pay-off made in some God-forsaken bit of the Pas de Calais? I really had no way of knowing. I would have to wait and see. I'd been given the map – presumably by Beag. Fine, I would let him tell me in his own good time what I was supposed to do with it.

From the studio, I called Captain Berry. I wanted to find out if he had made any progress in persuading his associates in the Irish Thoroughbred Breeders' Association to increase the re-ward. At that stage, I was convinced that the promise of more money was the one thing that was likely to loosen Beag's tongue and make him start to explain some of the mysteries.

When I reached Captain Berry, the news was far more promising than I had dared to hope for. He said he'd been in touch with a number of breeders and he was pretty certain that he could get the figure up to £100,000. He said he had to talk to some more breeders before he could give the final go-ahead, but he expected to be able to call me the next day and tell me that everything was set.

I was delighted. My first instinct was to call Superintendent

Murphy and suggest ways he might be able to exploit the new reward, but before I could settle down to doing that, I got myself caught up in yet another crazy Shergar story which came in from Ireland over the wires.

The Dublin *Evening Herald* was the source of the story and, at first, it sounded like a real breakthrough. The paper said it had been in contact with a man called Paul Hogan who worked for a security company in London. Hogan claimed that he had seen Shergar twice in France, and had taken photographs of him. According to the *Herald,* Hogan said the horse was in the hands of a syndicate which was using him for breeding in France and that they would return him once the season was over.

As with most of the Shergar stories that came winging into the news-room, it turned out to be a time-wasting hoax. I was suspicious as soon as I saw the name Hogan because I vaguely remembered that someone of that name had once called LBC with some crazy story and had been dismissed by us as a nutter.

Anyway, the whole story came to nothing, but whilst checking it out I did find time to talk to Jimmy Murphy and tell him about the chance of an increased reward. I suggested to him that if the Thoroughbred Breeders did announce a £100,000 reward, then he should try to grab some of the publicity to help his own investigation along.

Saturday, 30 April, was going to be a big day for racing. There were eight meetings in Britain and Ireland, including one at Phoenix Park. The papers would be full of racing coverage and the splash item would be the increase in the reward.

'You need a bit of incentive, like this,' I told him. 'Bring the press back into it. Bring the public back into it. Tell them everything you've been doing over the last two months, and make a new appeal for co-operation.'

I told him that if Captain Berry called me back on the Friday, I would be contacting the editors in Fleet Street and giving them a press release from the Thoroughbred Breeders. I suggested that if I called him back, to confirm that the go-ahead had been given, Murphy might make similar advance arrangements through Dublin Castle for a big Irish national press conference, saying he was delighted with the new reward offer and that the police were still committed to doing everything in their power to capture those responsible for the kidnapping. Murphy was very interested in the idea, but, as it turned out, the increase in reward was not to be.

Captain Berry contacted me the next day, and said he was still meeting opposition from some of the breeders. He would do some more talking at the Phoenix Park meeting on the Saturday, but it didn't look quite so hopeful. It was a bitter disappointment but there was nothing more I could do until Captain Berry had talked to the rest of the breeders.

Then, on the Saturday morning, Beag contacted me again. I went to Hornsey Lane and Beag sounded quite abrupt.

'Is there any news?'

'You mean news about the news,' I said, trying to lighten his tone a bit.

'Do you have any news?' Beag repeated sourly.

The intonation was clear enough. He wanted money and he was very irritated that there was no progress.

'Look, I'm stuck at the moment,' I said. 'No one seems to be doing anything. How is the person?'

'All right.'

He sounded as though he was speaking the truth, but I could also tell that money was all he was interested in.

I tried to explain to him that I felt I was being mucked about and that there were good signs one minute, which seemed to change overnight.

'I don't know where to go from here,' I said. 'To be honest, I'm not really getting much help from anyone.'

What I was saying was true enough. I'd had nothing back from the Irish Embassy to suggest that Dr Kennedy's efforts were leading anywhere. There was still a chance that Captain Berry could bring the other breeders into line, but I knew I could no longer count on it.

'Talk to Drion, Astor and Butcher,' Beag said suddenly.

I hesitated. 'I know who Drion is,' I said, 'but who are Astor and Butcher?'

'Talk to them,' Beag repeated. 'They might help you with the money.'

Before I could ask again who they were, Beag had hung up and I was left with yet another unexplained thread.

Later that day, I had the news that no £100,000 reward was going to come from the Thoroughbred Breeders' Association.

Chapter 10

Every journalist will know how I felt at that stage in the search for Shergar. There was an overwhelming temptation to give up – or at least to risk having the whole investigation fall in the water by giving James Beag an ultimatum. There was no doubt that I was being royally messed about. I'd gone on one complete wild-goose chase to Dublin which had resulted in an infuriating day hanging around Jury's Hotel. I'd been on another trip to Waterford which had been fascinating but which hadn't produced a single shred of hard evidence. I'd had God knows how many phone conversations with the mysterious Beag and he'd given me enough teasing hints to make any journalist froth at the mouth – without backing up a single one of them. Now, I had a fragment of a map, two new names, and no immediate prospect of raising a big enough reward to get Beag to open up. I'd also spent a lot of my own money and used up a lot of LBC's goodwill.

Logically, I *should* give Beag an ultimatum. He wanted money? Fine! I would try and get it for him, but before I took another step I wanted hard evidence that he knew what he was talking about – and that he could deliver Shergar, one way or the other, if the money were forthcoming.

Yet I couldn't avoid the feeling that if I did do the logical thing, and started to come on strong with Beag, it wasn't going to produce the result I wanted. In the worst scenario, he might get really pissed off and violent, and I didn't fancy having to look round every dark corner for months to come, wondering whether 'the boyos' or some such, were waiting for me.

More likely, though, Beag would simply break off his calls. In one way, that would be a blessing, but I was too concerned about Shergar to want to risk it. Looking back on it, I'm quite sure I wouldn't have let myself be given the runaround like that for anything less than a chance to bring the beautiful Shergar back alive. The thought of possibly being able to save his life, combined with a journalist's natural stubbornness to want to stay with a story no matter what, made me decide to press on with my investigation.

I rang Ballymany for what was beginning to seem like the four hundredth time and was told, yet again, that Monsieur Drion was not available. That left the two other names. I had no clue at all who Butcher was, so I decided to concentrate on 'Astor'. I assumed he meant Sir John (Jakie) Astor who, as far as I knew, was the member of the Astor family who was most closely connected with racing. I had never met him and didn't know how to contact him, so I asked the IRN political editor, Peter Allen, for ideas. He suggested writing care of the House of Lords, but that wasn't quick enough for me, so I phoned the House of Lords secretaries' office instead. I was told that he was on holiday and out of the country. I left a message and said that I would try again in a few days.

Next, I did a quick round robin of some syndicate members to see if there were any developments. In the process, I discovered that a letter had gone out from Ballymany to members of the syndicate recommending that they should get in touch with their insurance brokers. I hadn't yet fathomed the complexities of the Shergar insurance situation, so I didn't know if there was any special significance in that. I did learn from one Irish member, though, that within the syndicate the main resistance to increasing the reward was coming from the English members.

I talked next to Dr Kennedy, and on that front the news was all bad. Dr Kennedy told me that when he raised my queries with Dublin, he had been told that the Government's hands were tied as the Ballymany Stud and, particularly, Ghislain Drion, were treating the kidnapping as their affair. Dr Kennedy told me that he had sent a message to the Government saying he believed that the whole matter was being badly handled and recommending that the reward should be increased because of the growing concern of everyone in the horse-racing world, and especially of the bloodstock breeders.

More calls produced a few other titbits here and there. Among them, I learned that Ballymany had hired a firm to provide private policing but that their main job seemed to be to guard the Stud, and Drion, rather than to find the missing horse.

Finally, I called Captain Rogers and discovered that although he had managed to see Drion, he wasn't any happier about his relations with Ballymany than I was. Apparently, Drion had told Rogers that nothing at all was happening in the search for the missing horse. But what intrigued Rogers more was Drion's attitude.

'Drion behaves as though he isn't interested in getting the horse back,' Rogers said. 'Listening to him sometimes, he almost sounds as though he's been told he'll get the horse back eventually, but not if he says anything in the meantime.'

Knowing how well Rogers ran his own Airlie Stud, I could see why he would get exasperated with a man like Drion. Rogers was very much an action-orientated man. He'd told Drion he favoured a really big reward, possibly as much as a quarter of a million pounds, but Drion had expressed polite interest without any indication whatever that he planned to do anything about the suggestion, even to the extent of putting it to the other members of the syndicate.

My final call in the series was to a friend in the City who knew something about the finance and brokerage side of horse-dealing, and I asked him if he knew anyone called Butcher who might have some connection with Shergar. He suggested the name of one firm – Hine and Butcher – but that turned out to be a false trail.

Unfortunately, I didn't know it was the wrong firm when Beag's next call came. He rang my flat on Sunday morning, 8 May. I was due to go to Park Royal football ground to do a commentary on a charity football match in aid of the Heart Foundation. I didn't have much time, but I needed to talk to him, so when he gave the code signal for the Hornsey Lane call-box, I rushed up there as fast as I could.

When I got there, there was a girl in the box and she drove me crazy by staying in there for twenty-five minutes. She ignored all my efforts to get her out – and my cursing and swearing – but eventually, when she did leave, Beag came on the line.

Strangely for him, he began apologizing for hanging up so abruptly on the last call. I don't know why he bothered, since two thirds of his calls seemed to end that way, but it was rather a more promising start than usual!

'Those names I gave you,' he said. 'Did you find out anything from them?'

I told him Astor was away, Drion was still in his ivory tower and I hoped to talk to Butcher shortly. As I didn't know then I had the wrong Butcher, I didn't bother to ask Beag for more details.

He sounded disappointed.

'Tell me about the place you went to,' he said.

'You mean Waterford?' I asked.

'Yes.'

'Oh no,' I said quickly, '*you* tell *me*. Is the person all right and is he still in Ireland?'

'Yes. It's all right.'

'You didn't answer my other question,' I said. 'Is it still in Ireland?'

'I'm saying to you it doesn't matter,' Beag said. 'He's all right.'

'If he's not in Ireland, then you took him out through Waterford,' I said.

Beag didn't answer.

'Waterford definitely has some connection with this,' I insisted.

'Yes.'

'Has it some connection with the two strange men I found?' I asked.

Since I'd mentioned them tentatively to Beag on the previous call I'd done more checking, and I was now certain that European Electronics didn't exist.

'I don't know what two men you found,' Beag said.

'Look, for Christ's sake,' I said angrily, 'is the person out of Ireland? Is that the way you took it out?'

'I'm not saying that.' There was definitely an odd note to his voice. It wasn't an outright denial.

'If you're not saying that,' I said, 'it means you took him the other way, to the North. But there's still some connection with Waterford.'

I was thinking now about my other theory – that Waterford had been used as a conduit to ship arms into the IRA in payment for their help with the kidnap.

But Beag wasn't biting.

'All right, all right, all right,' he said.

He was beginning to sound irritated now, and I didn't know what to make of his answer. Presumably he was saying, 'Yes, Waterford was involved'. But we were still going round in circles.

'Look, what the hell do you want me to do?' I said.

'I told you already,' Beag said sharply. 'Talk to Drion, Astor and Butcher.'

'Let's get this straight,' I said. 'You want me to talk to them to get some reward money for you?'

'Yes.'

'Great,' I said. 'You tell me nothing, but you want me to get you some reward money, then you want to run off and leave me holding the fucking baby.'

'Yes.'

He said it almost humorously, but it wasn't really a joke, and there wasn't any warmth in his voice.

I tried to make it into a joke. 'If I were holding the real baby, that would make me a fucking millionaire,' I said.

But all Beag said was, 'So what. Eventually, someone will make a lot of money out of this.'

'Maybe,' I said, 'but it won't be me, because it's cost me a fortune already.'

'Someone will make money,' Beag repeated, 'even if it's only the insurance.'

Then, in his usual style, he changed the subject without any warning or apparent reason.

'Are you sure your phone isn't tapped?' he asked.

'I don't think so,' I said. 'But what the hell does it matter? They can tap my phone all they like. We don't talk on my phone.'

But I realized Beag was bringing up something he'd already decided about. He wanted to use another call-box and he said he had the number of one that would be O.K. It was in Parliament Hill Fields, and when he described it to me I recognized the box.

I wrote down the number and we agreed that he would add yet another set of two rings on to the signal.

'O.K.,' he said, when we had the details settled, 'I'll talk to you soon.'

Then he hung up.

In the week that followed, I talked briefly to Sir John Astor, but it didn't do me very much good. I eventually tracked him down at his home, once the House of Lords had confirmed that he was back from holiday. When he came on the line I introduced myself and told him I was very interested in the Shergar situation. Astor confirmed that he was a shareholder but he would say nothing.

'It's still being handled by Ghislain Drion, at Ballymany,' he said. 'I'd prefer not to get involved or make any statements.'

I couldn't make him change his mind and I didn't get anywhere near a position where I could start to talk about James Beag.

I had a second disappointment two days later when I called the Irish Embassy and was told, 'There is nothing whatever coming along.'

By now, I was beginning to feel that the whole situation was getting completely out of control. I was working that week on the LBC 'AM' London programme, presenting sport, which meant I was leaving the house at 3.30 a.m. So for virtually a whole week I wasn't around at the time I would normally expect Beag to call. I don't know whether he did try to call during that week, but he could well have, because he came through to my flat on the Monday – 16 May – immediately after my early shift had finished.

He used the latest signal and I went straight to the box he had chosen in Parliament Hill Fields. I didn't like the new location. It was only a small thing, but someone had broken a milk bottle right beside the box and a man was sweeping it up. I was very uptight, anyway, and I didn't like seeing someone so close to the box. My immediate thought was that it might be a set-up. After all, Beag had chosen this box. This was his ground, not mine. I waited for a moment until the broken pieces were swept up and the man moved away then, after looking round and seeing nothing else suspicious, I stepped into the box.

The phone rang almost immediately. I picked it up and Beag's anger almost took my breath away.

'Is there any reward yet?' he asked. His voice was hard, aggressive. Quite different from any of the previous calls.

'No,' I said, 'there's no reward.'

'Then talk to Drion.' There was real bitterness in his voice. 'God, I hate that fucker. Talk to him,' Beag said.

'He won't talk to me,' I said. 'I've told you that.'

'Talk to him. Talk to him about the reward. But talk to him alone.'

'What do you mean?'

'He's got an ex-SAS man. He's always with him. He's called Mike. Don't talk in front of him.'

'For Christ's sake,' I said, 'he won't talk to me. With this guy Mike or without him.'

Beag ignored my objection.

'Did you find the piece of paper,' he asked.

'In the wing mirror?'

'Yes.'

'What's that all about?' I queried. 'Is it important?'

'Yes.'

'Where does it fit in?'

'Drion will know. You've got to see Drion.'

'You want me to show him the map?'

'Yes. Show him.'

'Look, how many times have I told you,' I said angrily, 'Drion refuses to see anyone.'

'He'll talk,' Beag said. 'Interview the bastard. Find out what he has to say. Tell him you want to know if there's a reward and how much it is. Broadcast it in your programme. Tell him to do his own dealing. Tell him to take his own calls.'

'He won't tell me that. He won't say anything to me,' I said.

'He will, he'll talk. Tell him his time is running out.'

'Look, you tell me,' I said, 'is the person still all right?'

'It's all right,' Beag said. 'Just do what I'm telling you. Goodbye.'

I thought I was up against another blank wall but the next day I got a shock. I spent the morning interviewing Sheila Ferguson of Prince Charles's favourite pop group, The Three Degrees, for an hour-long special on IRN. Then I went back to the office and put in my umpteenth call to Ballymany. For once, it wasn't engaged and I spoke to Drion's secretary. I said that she knew I'd been trying to see Mr Drion for some time and now it was extremely urgent.

She said she would check, left me for three or four minutes, and then came back on the line.

'Monsieur Drion would like to see you,' she said. 'When would you be available?'

'I can see him any time, anywhere, in the next forty-eight to seventy-two hours.'

'Then let's say Thursday, 19 May at 11.00 a.m., here at Ballymany.'

'Yes,' I said. 'That's fine.'

I had no idea what had happened to change the situation, but finally I was going to be let in. I felt as though God had decided to open the gates of Heaven!

Chapter 11

The chance to see Drion was such a breakthrough that I was determined to keep it as close a secret as possible. As far as I knew, no other journalist had talked to him. In the early days, right after the kidnapping, one or two papers had carried stories which contained references to an 'interview' with Ghislain Drion, but when examined closely, they turned out to be a phone call to Ballymany, during which Monsieur Drion announced that he didn't know anything and had nothing to say. If word got out now that I was about to be ushered into the presence, I'd be arriving at Ballymany with the entire British and Irish press corps sitting on my tail.

As it happened, it wasn't to be a problem. By pure good luck, the perfect cover for my trip to Ireland had already been arranged. Wednesday, 18 May, the day before I was due to go to Ballymany, was the draw for the Daily Mirror Greyhound Derby. The draw for the 170 entries was due to be made at lunch-time in a snooker club near the *Daily Mirror* offices in Holborn, and I had been invited to make it, as I do quite a lot of presentations for the Mirror Group.

There is a tremendous Irish interest in the race and seventy or seventy-five percent of all the greyhounds running in Britain are Irish-bred. The Greyhound Derby is the classic of the sport and the *Daily Mirror* was sponsoring it for the first time, taking it over from Spillers, the pet food people.

Because of the Irish interest, the Mirror Group had asked me to fly over to Dublin immediately after the draw, together with the other members of the presentation team, Ray Lancaster, one of the *Mirror*'s editorial managers, and John Willis, who is in change of promotions, to host a reception at the Gresham Hotel in Dublin for the Irish greyhound press.

After the final press conference at the *Mirror* offices in London, I was whisked over to Dublin and was chatting to the greyhound press by five o'clock in the afternoon. Thanks to Joe Kennedy, the director of operations for Bord Failte, and Keith Pope, the manager of the Gresham Hotel, everything went off smoothly. The next day, unnoticed, I slipped away, rented a Hertz car and drove down to Newbridge, to the Ballymany Stud.

I entered the gates of Ballymany at exactly five-minutes-to-eleven, and drove up the long avenue leading to the stud buildings, past the now deserted caravan which had been used as a police operations centre after the kidnap. Taking my tape-recorder and brief-case with me, I went into the small one-storey building with 'Office' printed on its glass door.

Inside, in a dark hallway-cum-reception area, I found a low-sized man with glasses who greeted me with a very strong French accent. I told him I was Colin Turner and that I had an appointment to see Monsieur Drion.

'Oh yes,' he said. 'Monsieur Drion is on the phone at the moment.'

I waited for about ten minutes and I spent the time reviewing Drion's sins. I knew it was going to be a sticky interview. One thing that had stood out through all the mysterious phone calls, was that James Beag didn't have a very high opinion of Ghislain Drion, and I must say that, quite independently, I had come to the same conclusion. So, too, it seemed, had Murphy, Captain Rogers and Captain Berry.

As manager of the Stud, he had to take responsibility for the fact that the camera in the stallion barn where Shergar was boxed was not working – and according to my own information, that was only one aspect of very lax security arrangements at Ballymany.

I'm the first to admit that there's no tradition of barbed-wire fences, watch-towers and security patrols at studs in Ireland, but Ballymany did seem to have gone to the other extreme. Ironically, I'd heard from a very reliable source that about two months before the kidnap, Drion had been offered an excellent security system for the Stud but he had turned it down because its cost – £1,000 – was too high!

Drion himself lived at the Aga Khan's other Irish establishment, the Sheshoon Stud, three or four miles from Ballymany, on the other side of the Curragh, and at the time of the kidnap the only people on the premises at Ballymany were the Fitzgerald family, in their cottage at least 500 yards from Shergar's barn.

Then there was the crucial question of the delay in notifying the police. The timetable, as I understood it, was that the groom, Jimmy Fitzgerald, had been released by the kidnappers at Kilcock at about twelve-past-midnight. His brother, Des, had arrived to pick him up at about half-past-twelve. They had called Drion immediately, so he had known about the kidnap by 12.45 a.m., more than four hours before Superintendent Murphy was notified.

Instead of notifying the police, Drion's first contact with the Irish authorities was a phone call to Alan Dukes, the Minister of Finance, whom he had met not long before. Poor Dukes. It was his first Budget Day since becoming Finance Minister, but instead of getting his beauty sleep before the big day in the Dail (the Irish Parliament), he was woken at about 4.30 a.m. to be told that thieves had made off with what – to a horse-loving nation like the Irish – amounted to a priceless treasure which had been placed temporarily in their custody!

There was a lot more I might have been thinking about Drion, but my main worry was not what I could say to him, but what he would say to me. If he refused to co-operate in any way, I could well be at the end of the road with Beag, and Shergar's death sentence might have been passed.

At last I was shown into Drion's office. Drion stood to greet me, and my first impression of the Aga Khan's stud manager was that he was the wrong nationality! Ghislain Drion looked more like an English Guards officer than a French racing man. He was big and very striking, standing about six feet three inches at his full height, and straight-backed with it. With him in the same room, standing unobtrusively at one side, was a much shorter man of about five feet eight inches, with sandy hair, and dressed in a loose pullover. Drion didn't introduce him.

'Well, Mr Turner,' Drion said, as I went in. 'What can we do for you?'

We sat down, Drion behind a big office desk covered with papers, me in a visitor's chair facing him and the unknown man

97

at a desk in the corner, disconcertingly behind my back and out of my line of vision.

'Monsieur Drion,' I said, 'we have many things to talk about. I've been trying for months to see you.'

'I'm sorry,' Drion said. 'I've been very busy.'

'Could I ask why you have agreed to see me now, when you refused for so long?'

But Drion ducked the question. 'It was not possible until now,' was all he said.

'Monsieur Drion, I have been asked to come and see you,' I went on. 'I'll explain how it came about, but I'd like to ask first if this gentleman,' I turned to indicate the man behind me, 'will be present during our conversation?'

'Oh yes,' Drion said, in a very off-handed way. 'This is Mike. He is one of my associates. He always stays during my meetings.'

I decided to bite the bullet.

'Then I'd better tell you, Monsieur Drion, that I have been warned in advance about this gentleman. The man who asked me to come and see you told me not to talk to you in front of anyone else.'

Drion tried to brush my objection aside. 'But Mike is just an associate. He works with me. It makes no difference that he is here.'

'That's not the way I heard it,' I said. 'I was told that you have your own private police force working for you here in Ireland, which is illegal, and that one of them is a former SAS man. Is he the one?'

Drion didn't answer. I knew the interview might blow up in my face there and then but, I thought, what the hell? I might as well stick to the script that Beag had laid out for me.

Drion and Mike exchanged strong glances, then Drion said, 'I told you, Mr Turner, Mike is a business associate. He is not a policeman.'

No, I thought, and I'm not a racing correspondent either, but I let it pass.

'Monsieur Drion,' I said, 'I'm just repeating to you what I was told. If he's to stay during our conversation, that's all right with me. I'm passing on what my contact said. So is he staying?'

'Yes,' Drion said. 'He will stay.'

I had realized by now that Drion was distinctly wary of me, maybe even a bit scared. I think he wasn't sure whether I really was the journalist I was supposed to be. I think he thought he might be dealing with one of the kidnap gang, a member of the IRA, or some such. And I really think he wanted Mike there for protection. I didn't want to continue the argument and risk losing my chance to talk. I didn't like having Mike there, behind my back, but it was obvious that I was going to have to live with it.

'Tell me about this man who told you to see me,' Drion said. 'What is he like?'

'He's O.K. He seems to know what he's talking about.'

'So you have met him?'

'I've never met him,' I said. 'He's been contacting me by telephone.'

'How does he contact you?'

The interruption came from Mike, behind me, and I could see I was in for a double interrogation.

I explained that we had a system of signals to identify his calls, though I didn't say what they were, and I gave them both the minimum information possible about how the calls were made, and what the voice was like.

'The important thing about the calls is,' I said, 'that this man has been giving me good information. I don't need to ask you whether he was telling me the truth. I've already checked his stories out with the police and other contacts and I can tell you that he knows what's been going on.'

Drion wanted every single detail of what Beag had told me, and I gave him quite a lot of it, starting with the information about the horse-box colour. By the time we got to the bit about Flight 208, and the payment of the confidence money, Drion was giving me some very old-fashioned looks. He looked puzzled at first, and when I spelled out the details of what Beag had said – about the flight delay and the shipments of money going on board and being taken off in Paris – he denied that he knew anything about such events. His expression showed shock and surprise, but perhaps what was shocking him was that I knew about all this.

Gradually, Drion exhausted his preliminary questions about Beag and we came finally to the crucial one.

99

'What does this man want?' Drion asked.

'First of all, he wants money,' I said. 'He wants a reward for information. And he wants more than there is on offer already. He told me to talk to you to get a bigger reward put out. I believe this man is on the fringe of the gang. I think he's a weak link, who will sell the others out if reward money is put up. But he wants something else.' I said.

I pointed down at the tape-recorder at my feet.

'He wants you to do an interview with me, saying what the situation is. He wants you to talk about the reward. He wants it in your voice. He says you should do your own dealing. Not hide behind other people.'

During our conversation Drion had glanced several times at the tape-recorder. I had brought my big machine and it looked more like a flight-bag, or camera holdall, than a recording machine, and I could tell Drion wasn't sure what it was.

'That is a recorder?' he asked edgily.

'Yes,' I said. 'But it isn't turned on. It's there for you to do an interview with me about the reward.'

'There is nothing I can do about the reward without consulting other members of the syndicate,' he said. 'I am only the manager here.'

'That's great,' I said. 'Every time I talk to the members of the syndicate, they tell me to talk to you, because you're in charge. You're controlling everything. Now, you say, you're not.'

'I will have to talk to them,' Drion said stubbornly.

'Well, at least do an interview,' I said. 'Speak with your own voice. Do what my contact asks. Give an interview on the situation as it is now. Not a rehash of the story of the kidnap. People want to know what's happening *now*. Look, I'm a competitive journalist, but if you'll do this interview I won't keep it just for myself. I'll offer it to the other radio and television networks: the BBC, ITV, RTE, and all the papers. I'll get it the widest possible distribution I can. I think my contact can help us get the horse back. I don't think you have the right not to make use of him. Just do the interview. Start being frank with people for a change.'

'I would have to talk to the other members of the syndicate,' Drion repeated. 'I could not do that on my own.'

'Of course you can,' I said. 'Never mind for the moment

about increasing the reward. I agree that might take time, but you could do it. You could get the other members of the syndicate to put up, say, £3,000 or £4,000 each. I know some who are willing already. There are thirty-four shareholders altogether. You could get more than enough. But in the mean-time, just tell people what the situation is now. Break down this wall of silence you've built round Ballymany.'

'You are asking for the impossible,' Drion said. 'You told me that some members you have talked to would put up £3,000 or £4,000 each as their share of a bigger reward. But I can tell you, Monsieur Turner, one member of the syndicate sat in that chair you are sitting in now, and told me he would not pay *three* or *four* pounds to get the horse back.'

I wasn't getting anywhere, so I decided it was time for shock tactics. I reached down and opened my brief-case.

'Monsieur Drion,' I said, 'may I introduce something else into our conversation?'

I took a photocopy of the fragment of map out of my brief-case and laid it on the table in front of me.

'What can you tell me about this?' I said.

'What is it?'

'It's a map.'

Drion got up from his chair and came round to my side of the table to look at it. Mike, who had been sitting quietly behind me taking no part in the conversation, came over too, and started to examine it.

'This is strange. Very strange altogether,' Drion said.

'I was told to ask you about the map,' I said.

'Who told you?'

'The man on the phone.'

'Where did you get the map?' Drion asked.

'The man gave it to me.'

Drion seized on the point immediately. 'So you have seen this man,' he said excitedly. 'You have met him. What is he like? Who is he?'

'No, I haven't met him,' I said. 'He put the map in the wing-mirror of my car, then talked to me about it on the phone later.'

'No. You must have met him,' Drion said.

I repeated in great detail how I had come by the map in the station car park at King's Cross, but I could see Drion didn't

101

believe me, and I guessed Mike didn't either.

'The map is somewhere in France,' I said. 'You should know about it. You're supposed to know about this.'

Drion studied the map for a few minutes.

'What can you tell me about it?' I prompted.

'Yes, it is France, as you say,' Drion said. 'I know the area. I know it very well.'

'So what does it mean to you?' I asked.

'It means nothing.'

I pointed at the map. 'If you look closely,' I said, 'you'll see there's a mark on it.'

Drion went back to his desk drawer, got a magnifying glass, and examined the map minutely. Mike took it too, looking at it all ways up and holding it up to the light.

'I can see the mark,' Drion said. 'I know this place.'

'So what does it mean?' I said.

'I don't know. It means nothing.'

While they were examining the map through the magnifying glass, Drion also found a second mark which I had not seen. Like the other, it seemed to be in the middle of nowhere, rather than in a town or a village, and again Drion denied knowing what it meant.

Eventually, I began to lose patience with Drion's stalling. I'd done exactly what Beag had told me to do and I'd brought Drion information that could only be valuable to him as the Chairman of the syndicate committee handling the search for Shergar, but he was obviously prepared to give me absolutely nil co-operation in return. And that really got my goat. To hell with Mike, I thought, and to hell with all this polite farting about. Let's see if a few home truths will have any effect.

'Monsieur Drion,' I said, 'my contact says you're not handling things right and I have to say that I agree with him. In fact, to put it bluntly, I think you're cocking things up.'

'What do you mean?' Drion put down the map, looking angry – and more than a bit surprised.

'You're doing too many things wrong,' I said. 'If you had taken the newspapers into your confidence from the beginning we could have flushed the kidnappers out by now. But never mind the press, you're not even taking the police into your confidence.'

'Yes we are,' Drion said. 'We are in touch with the police.'

'You may be in touch with them,' I said bitterly, 'but you don't tell them a God-damn thing. How the hell can the police catch the kidnappers if you don't pass on information to the man in charge?'

'That's not true.'

'Yes it is,' I said. 'You talked to Superintendent Murphy a couple of times at the beginning and since then, if he wants anything he has to come to you, and then he gets damn all. You're busy playing power games. Talking to your friends in the Irish Government. But it isn't them that need information. It's the people like Murphy who are out there looking for the horse. You've brought in your own private police force, which is illegal in Ireland, and you're carrying on in your own little world, shutting out everyone who can help you. You haven't talked to Captain Sean Berry of the Irish Thoroughbred Breeders. He's been getting all his information from the vet, Stan Cosgrove. The only thing *you'll* catch is a cold if you don't talk to the people who matter. I've talked to Lord Derby, Sir John Astor, Jonathan Irwin, Captain Berry and Superintendent Murphy. Stan Cosgrove refuses to see me, and I've talked to European and American members of the syndicate, and all of them are very concerned about the handling of the situation.'

'We're doing all we can,' Drion said.

'Fine,' I said. 'And if the royal "we" is supposed to mean that all the members of the syndicate are doing their bit, why hasn't His Royal Highness the Aga Khan set foot in Ireland since the kidnap?'

'There is no need for that. We are leaving that to the police.'

'No you're not,' I said. 'You're not helping the police at all. If HRH had flown over to Ireland and been seen standing outside Naas police station with Jimmy Murphy, the Irish people would have done everything possible to help. But here we are, fourteen weeks after the kidnap, and the Aga Khan hasn't done a single thing to show the people of Ireland that he's concerned. You must remember this is a country where the people love their animals. Schoolkids could tell you who Monksfield and Arkle were, quicker than they could name the disciples.'

It was about this point in the row that I suddenly realized that

103

Mike was no longer with us. He'd just slipped out quietly. I had no idea what he was up to, but by this time I didn't care. I'd really lost my temper with Monsieur Ghislain Drion and I felt it was about time someone told him how he appeared to the outside world.

'You say you're leaving everything to the police,' I continued, 'but tell me straight. When was the last time you picked up the phone and talked to Jimmy Murphy? Murphy needs all the help he can get and, as far as I can see, he isn't getting any from here.'

Several times during my outburst, Drion tried to break it off but, unless he was going to throw me out physically, I'd no intention of stopping.

'My man on the phone keeps saying to do your own dealing,' I said. 'Now you've got your chance. Do the interview with me. Make a statement that shows you really are as concerned as you tell me you are. Get the media and the people behind you.'

'I told you, I have to talk to the others,' Drion said yet again.

'Your job is to keep the lines of communication open,' I said. 'The other members of the syndicate are counting on you to do that. It happens in every kidnapping, whether it's IRA, or Red Brigade or Baader Meinhof. If anything is going to happen, you have to keep communications open. You're doing everything you can to shut them down.'

I was, of course, referring to my lines of communication.

'Monsieur Turner, we have to agree to disagree,' Drion said. 'I will think about the things you have told me. They are all very interesting. I will be in touch with you.'

'Monsieur Drion,' I said, 'if one of the kidnappers walked in here, by the time you'd got your instructions from HRH or talked to the Irish Government, he'd have walked out again and got on a bus. You all seem to be pissing about.'

Eventually, I cooled down a bit and Drion tried again to persuade me to leave. I agreed, but only after I'd received a solemn assurance from him that he would be in touch very soon. We decided that I would stay in Ireland until he did. I gave him all the phone numbers where I could be contacted. Drion said again and again that he *would* be in touch. He understood the urgency, he said. He knew that my contacts with Beag were an opportunity that had to be exploited. He also wanted me to send

104

him the real map, not the photocopy I had shown to him, but I refused.

'It's in the vault of a bank in London,' I said. But I let him keep the photocopy.

At least I left under my own steam, not on the toe of Mike's boot, but as I drove down the long avenue towards the gates of Ballymany, I admit I was thoroughly dejected. I read Drion as a man who was incapable of decisive action. He hadn't even stood up for himself while I was hurling insults at him. He was even talking about getting instructions from others while I was telling him to his face how useless everyone thought he was!

But I had his promise that he would be in touch very soon. As I drove towards Dublin, I knew that all I could do for the moment was to wait. It was to be the longest wait of my professional life.

Chapter 12

From Ballymany, I drove straight to Naas police headquarters for a long chat with Superintendent Jimmy Murphy. My meeting with Drion had been so unsatisfactory that I decided it would be a good idea to bring Murphy up-to-date on the situation – and to tell him a few things about Ballymany that he probably didn't know, given the appalling communications between Drion and the police.

The meeting with Murphy had none of the formality of our first interview. I felt he had accepted me – and I'm sure he'd done some checking up on my background since I first started to talk to him. It was easy to brief him in a very casual, relaxed way. I didn't tell him everything that had passed between myself and Drion, but I told him most of it – certainly enough for him to have a clear picture of what I was up to and trying to achieve.

Looking back, two points stand out from our conversation that day. The first concerned the times during the interview with Drion when he had spoken about 'dealing with the police'. I didn't know whether he had meant the Garda or his own people – all of which Murphy found very strange.

The second point concerned the map. I showed a photocopy of the map to Murphy, and eventually left it with him. Murphy was fascinated by it and said it meant nothing to him at all; there had been no reference to this part of France at any time during his investigation. Murphy asked me what Drion's reaction had been. I said the sight of the map had given him a bit of a shock, and he'd admitted knowing the area, but denied knowing what it meant.

After we'd talked some more about how I'd got hold of the map in the first place, Murphy asked me what connection *I* thought it had with the Shergar affair. I had to say that I didn't know, but when Murphy asked me to speculate, and make an informed guess, I said I thought the connection might well be with the payment of the confidence money and the business of Gulf Air Flight 208.

I reminded Murphy that, according to Beag, the money had been loaded onto the flight which was going from London to the Middle East, but had been taken off in Paris. Could the mark on the map have been the rendezvous with the kidnappers where the money was actually paid over? It was certainly a possibility, and Murphy said he would do some investigating of his own.

After this very frank conversation with Murphy I drove back to Dublin, and there my frustrations began.

I spent the whole of the next day – 20 May – hanging around the Gresham Hotel in Dublin waiting for Drion's call. When the day began, I had no doubt that Drion would get in touch. I wasn't certain what he would say – there was obviously no guarantee that he would give me the interview – but he had made great play of giving me his absolute, unconditional assurance that he would contact me.

By lunch-time no call had come, and I was beginning to get a bit edgy. By mid-afternoon, there was still nothing, and I was now really frustrated and more than a little angry. At twenty-past-four, I called Ballymany and couldn't get through. After leaving careful messages with the hotel switchboard, I walked down to Eason's Bookstore. But even a stroll around one of my favourite hunting-grounds couldn't ease my gloom and frustration.

When I got back to the hotel, there was still no message for me from Drion, so I called Ballymany. This time I spoke to a woman in the office, who told me that Monsieur Drion was not available. I'm afraid I really let her have it. I told her what I thought of Drion and his manners and told her to remind him that he had guaranteed me absolutely that he would be in touch.

'Monsieur Drion must have forgotten the call,' she said. 'He is away for the week-end. I am positive he will contact you on Monday.'

Needless to say, no call came through for the rest of the day. I called the Irish Embassy in London, intending to brief Dr Kennedy about the situation, but he wasn't available. Still with no word from Ballymany, I had no choice but to return to

London.

I was still hopeful that Drion would eventually contact me. I was furious that he had broken his word, but some news on Monday would not be too late. I had given the woman in the Ballymany office the details of my movements and all my contact numbers right up to Wednesday and Thursday.

On the Monday, back in London, I called Dr Kennedy and told him that I was staying at home throughout the day to wait for news from Drion about whether the syndicate would put up a reward. I told him about the interview with Drion and my meeting with Murphy, and I also mentioned the map. Kennedy was now right up-to-date; he had no news on any reward from the Government side, but he wished me luck with the syndicate and Drion.

While I was at the flat killing time, I called Duncan Campbell, a journalist on the *New Statesman* who specializes in phone tapping and issues such as the citizen's right to privacy. Beag's concern about my phone being tapped had made me start to wonder, too, and I wanted to ask Campbell the legal position. He wasn't available at the time but later that night I told him that it was possible that my phone was being tapped and asked him what I should do.

'Don't use it,' was Campbell's blunt advice. 'In fact,' he added, 'don't even use the same phone-box over and over again if you're worried about taps.'

I said, perhaps naïvely, 'But don't they need permission from the Home Office before they tap your phone?'

Campbell's answer was again direct, and hardly reassuring.

'Yes,' he said. 'That's right. They do need permission. But no government in the world ever sticks to the rules.'

By this time, I was already eaten up with frustration at not having heard from Drion, and Campbell's remarks didn't do much to cheer me up. The reality, I suppose, was that only a call from Ballymany would have done any good, and though I had waited patiently by my phone for the whole of Monday, there was still no call.

On Tuesday (the 24th), I was due to attend one of the most enjoyable social events in the racing calendar – The Piper Champagne Awards luncheon at the Dorchester Hotel. I had even left that number with Drion's secretary, so that he would have no excuse for not reaching me there, and I went to the lunch and tried to put Drion out of my mind for a few hours, at least.

The lunch was a very splendid affair, as always, but especially so this year as the guests of honour were Prince Charles and Princess Diana. The guest-list was a catalogue of the top people in racing, the food was delightful and the atmosphere greatly helped by the free flow of Piper Heidsieck champagne! It could have been a very enjoyable diversion after several days of acute frustration, but even at the Dorchester there was no escape from Shergar.

During the lunch I received a message passed on to me by the office. At first, when I was paged, I thought, if only for a moment, that Drion had finally got in touch. But it turned out to be an urgent request to call Dr Eamonn Kennedy, the Irish Ambassador. When I made the call, I didn't know what to expect. It wasn't like Dr Kennedy's secretary to have the office break into a function like the National Hunt Awards lunch, and I wondered whether, despite the initially poor reaction, the Irish Government had finally agreed to put up a reward. It could be that, though there were a number of other matters the Ambassador might be calling about.

But when I made the call to the Embassy and asked for Dr Kennedy, I was in no way prepared for the bombshell that was to come. When the Ambassador came on the line, he sounded distinctly worried.

'Colin,' he said, 'have you seen *The Irish Press* today?'

'No,' I said, 'I'm afraid I haven't had the time. What's happening?'

'There's a rather disturbing story,' Dr Kennedy said. 'I think it may concern you. I just wanted to make sure you're all right.'

Dr Kennedy gave me a quick outline of the story and I stood, holding the phone, completely flabbergasted. Not only had Monsieur Drion not kept his word and called me back, but, if the *France Soir* report was accurate, Drion had apparently given an interview which could have had serious consequences for me.

I raced back to the office, found a copy of *The Irish Press*, and read the story in full. I don't know whether Drion realized it, but as far as my relations with Beag were concerned, the report, true or not, was dynamite. 'SECRET "TALKS IN FRANCE" ON

SHERGAR DEAL' the headline read, over a story bylined by Paddy Butler, an old friend of mine. This is what it said:

The Aga Khan has received death threats over his refusal to negotiate with the kidnappers of Shergar, according to a report in the *France Soir* newspaper, which also stated that secret talks were going on about a ransom for the stallion.

French police are said to be angry that senior Garda officers who carried out investigations into the stallion's disappearance, visited France secretly and failed to alert the authorities here, the report stated.

The threats were reportedly passed on to the French police ten days ago by the French director of the Ballymany Stud. The Director, Mr Ghislain Drion, also told police that fresh ransom talks were taking place in France, the report added.

According to the newspaper, the Aga Khan was told by the kidnappers, 'Shergar will be mutilated or killed. Everyone involved in the ransom talks will be liquidated.'

Racing and bloodstock circles in Ireland were surprised last night by the report. One source welcomed the news as an indication that the horse was still alive.

Mr Drion is in France and could not be contacted for comment on the story last night. However, his wife, speaking from Ballymany, discounted the report that fresh ransom talks were taking place.

She said her husband left Kildare on Saturday to attend the Longchamp races.

Gardai in Newbridge know of no fresh developments in the kidnapping. A spokesman for the Garda Press Office, asked to comment on the 'secret visit', said that no Gardai were in France in connection with the investigation lately.

Captain Sean Berry of the Irish Thoroughbred Breeders' Association, which offered a reward for information, said he had heard nothing about the new French moves.

However, Mr Jonathan Irwin, of Goff's the bloodstock dealers, saw the French report as a welcome indication that the horse could still be alive and well. 'I have always been convinced that Shergar is still alive,' he said last night.

In the light of my situation at the time, the story was really appalling. Leaving aside the possibility that it had been concocted as pure fantasy by *France Soir,* it had to have come, in some form or other, from Drion. I would have been astonished to learn that he had talked to the French police ten days previously. If he had, no one in the syndicate that I had spoken to knew about it, and he had given no indication of the fact to me in our meeting. As far as I knew, I was the only person who had brought France into the picture – by telling Drion what Beag had said in connection with the confidence money and Flight 208, and by giving him the map of part of France.

If Beag saw the story – as he surely would – it would look as though I had been passing on threats to the Aga Khan which he had not made. At the time I believed I was the only person who could have been referred to as being involved in 'fresh ransom talks'. As far as anyone knew – and certainly as far as Jimmy Murphy knew – there had been the phone call two days after the kidnap, confirming the original two-million-pound ransom demand. Then, apart from hoaxes, university rag stunts and the like, mine was the first serious contact with an apparent member of the gang. Could Drion have been doing his best to set me up? I found that hard to believe of the fellow.

I was vulnerable on two fronts. Beag would probably believe that I was playing my own games, instead of trying to help him as I had promised to do. And I was vulnerable from the rest of the media and the authorities. The Ambassador's first thought had been to call me, as he had assumed that the map, and my conversation with Drion, were connected with the story and that I was being named as the intermediary in the 'fresh talks' – complete with their threats of death and mutilation.

If someone as intelligent and perceptive as Dr Kennedy could jump to the conclusion that I was being set up, then I really was in trouble. If any of my colleagues found out that I was the last person to talk to Ghislain Drion, then my life was going to be hell, since Fleet Street – apparently scooped by *France Soir* and *The Irish Press* – would go absolutely hysterical trying to use me to get a better story.

I had reassured Dr Kennedy that I could handle the situation, but as I read and re-read the story, I wasn't so sure. I phoned Ballymany and got the usual runaround. The situation there had reverted to the stonewalling that had gone on before my conversation with Drion. Another door had slammed shut. Even if I did manage to persuade Beag that I had not broken *my* word, I was still getting nowhere in my efforts to raise a reward.

'See Drion, Astor, Butcher,' Beag had said. 'They'll help you.' Astor had refused to even discuss the issue and I had the impression that Drion would like me to take a long holiday! That left 'Butcher', a man I wasn't even sure existed.

During my conversation with Drion at Ballymany, I had mentioned to him that Beag had ordered me to see him (Drion), and Astor and Butcher. Drion knew Sir John Astor, of course, but he had said he had never heard of Butcher, and my own enquiries weren't getting very far.

The lead to Hine and Butcher had turned out to be a dead end; there was no Butcher there who had any connection whatever with Shergar. Another contact had suggested I try a firm of solicitors, Ruston and Lloyd in Newmarket, but I had chatted to Mr Ratcliffe there, who hadn't been able to help. He confirmed that his firm had set up the original syndicate to buy Shergar when the Aga Khan had put the stallion up for sale at the time he was due to go to stud. Since then, Mr Ratcliffe said, neither he nor his firm had had anything to do with the horse. It was another dead-end, and I still hadn't found 'Butcher'.

When I did find him – through other contacts in the part of the City that is interested in bloodstock – he invited me immediately to come and see him, and it was a very odd meeting. We sat opposite each other, in Mr Butcher's office in Seething Lane in the City – with neither of us having the faintest idea why we were seeing the other.

The 'Butcher' that Beag had ordered me to contact turned out to be Mr James Butcher, the managing director of Butcher and Hall, the Lloyds insurance underwriters who had handled much of the insurance cover on Shergar. He was a courteous man in his mid-fifties, dressed in a dark suit. He was very open and honest with me, and gave a striking impression of knowing his business inside out. The problem was that he didn't know what the hell I was up to, nor did I know where he fitted in.

After an exchange of pleasantries, Mr Butcher opened the conversation by asking, 'Well, Mr Turner, what can I do for you?'

To his astonishment, I had to answer, 'I'm afraid I don't

know.'

I said I had been told to come and see him. Without going into precise details, I told him about Beag. I said that over several weeks he been giving me information which was turning out to be accurate, and he wanted a reward for further information. I explained that he had so far given me only teasing, unconnected scraps of information, but I said I had the feeling that he really did know where Shergar was, alive or dead, and would be willing to sell that information, even if it meant selling out the other members of the gang, for a suitable reward.

I described how Beag had said 'See Drion, Astor and Butcher', and how he had refused to explain who 'Butcher' was, leaving me to find out for myself. I told him that during my interview in Ballymany, Drion had denied any knowledge of Shergar's principal insurers, or knowing who Butcher was. Butcher was very surprised at this, but said it was possible that Drion had dealt with documents signed mainly by his partner, Mr Hall.

I then asked Butcher to explain how the insurance cover for Shergar was organized, and discovered that it was a great deal more complicated than I had anticipated.

Patiently, Mr Butcher outlined the complexities of the Lloyds underwriting process. The syndicate which *owns* the horse (in this instance) goes to a Lloyds broker, who will act for it, and the broker goes onto the floor of Lloyds, where the underwriters are – in this case to Mr Butcher's 'box' – and announces that he wants to insure Shergar. The broker and the underwriter negotiate for the sum to be insured and checks are carried out to make sure the horse is in good health and there are no veterinary problems.

The insurance itself, however, is eventually spread among other Lloyds underwriters because the sum insured on an animal like Shergar is too much for any one insurance syndicate. There are about 20,000 'names' at Lloyds, grouped into syndicates. Mr Butcher, as manager of the underwriting syndicate which agrees to insure Shergar, has the task of persuading individuals and syndicates to accept a portion of the risk. His overall role, as managing agent of the underwriting syndicate, is to make sure the syndicate's underwriting is properly conducted, records are kept, funds managed correctly and to carry

113

out, in short, all the functions of someone running a conventional insurance business.

In the case of Shergar, however, there are even further complications. When Shergar had gone to stud, he had been 'syndicated' (sold in effect) for ten million pounds, divided into forty shares of £250,000 each. The Aga Khan himself had retained six shares, and was still the biggest single owner in the syndicate (the owning syndicate), even though his holding amounted to only fifteen percent. Some buyers had bought a quarter of a million pound share outright, while others had formed special companies with other individuals to enable them to buy half a share.

There was another, very significant, group of syndicate members who had bought a whole quarter of a million pound share from the Aga Khan but had agreed to pay for it in 'hire purchase' instalments, plus interest, to him.

Mr Butcher explained that it was up to each owner of a share to organize his own insurance. He was not willing to discuss individuals' actual insurance dealings, but I gathered from him – and later from others – that the Aga Khan had insured his own shares, and had at the same time insured all the shares of those people buying by instalments, obliging the 'hire purchasers' to pay the premiums.

Some of the owners had not insured at all, while some others had insured against theft, but not against death, or vice versa. In rough terms, I gathered that between seven and eight million pounds of the horse's ten million pound syndicate value was covered by some form of insurance.

We then came down to the thorny question of a reward for James Beag. That was, after all, why I had been sent 'to see Butcher'. I asked him whose decision it would be to put up an insurance reward.

'The decision would have to be taken by the leading underwriters listening to their advisers,' Mr Butcher said.

When I asked whether it was true that rewards were always paid when the property lost was valuable enough, Mr Butcher said rewards were usually offered, except in the case of international terrorist activities, but strictly on the basis that the information given would lead to the recovery of the property and the conviction of the person who had taken it.

'It's pretty heavily qualified,' Mr Butcher said.

He also indicated that there was another complication affecting both payment of the insurance claims and the offer of rewards. He said he was not completely clear about the details but he understood there was a possibility that a claim might be made against the Irish Government under an ancient 'Public Order Act'.

There had been a fair amount of gossip about this already in racing circles. Apparently, there is a law in Ireland dating back to the early nineteenth century under which the police are required to maintain peace and order. If they fail to maintain it, and the result is riot or malicious damage, the civil authorities are liable to make good any damage caused. There had been a lot of jokes about it, too, as I'd been told that the actual lawsuit would have to be filed not against the Dublin Government, but against the Kildare County Council. The Council would have to do more than leave the streets in darkness if it ended up having to pay out for the loss of Shergar!

Once again, it was time to be direct. I told Butcher that these problems and complications were all very fine but I had a very simple and immediate problem. I believed that I had a man out there somewhere who might very well be able to get Shergar back alive and well for £100,000 or £150,000. I said I thought he might be delighted to take that kind of money and get out of the whole deal, skedaddle off to Spain, buy a cottage and leave us to get the horse – and maybe the rest of the gang, too, for all he cared.

I said I had been to the Irish Government, through the Ambassador, Dr Kennedy. I'd been to the bloodstock breeders and I'd been to several syndicate members. I'd also seen Drion, and that had been another dead-end. As far as I could see, Lloyds were about to have to pay out several million pounds on the horse and they could well save themselves that money by acting decisively and quickly now.

'What have you got to lose?' I asked. 'The money might never be paid over. No information might come, but no one has ever tried offering a serious reward.'

I said I believed we were dealing with an international gang, not the IRA or the INLA – although they could well have had a part in it. I said the motive might have been revenge on the Aga

115

Khan, who had a great many enemies throughout the world, but all of that mattered less than actually getting the horse back. I felt there was a chance to do that – acting through James Beag – and it was criminally stupid not at least to give it a try.

I made it very clear to Butcher that I was not just looking for a newspaper story – in fact, I'd turned down dozens of opportunities to broadcast or sell my information to Fleet Street for thousands of pounds. I'd done the investigating at my own expense and I seemed to be the only person who was taking the trouble to investigate properly, apart from the police – which in itself was surprising as, I said, I thought there would have been a very high-powered insurance investigation going on at the same time.

The end of our conversation will come as a surprise to no one. Mr Butcher was as courteous at the end of the interview as he had been at the beginning.

'It's a fascinating story,' he said. 'I'd like some time to assimilate it. I will get back to you. Can we leave it like that?'

Chapter 13

It was time to take stock. It was more than fourteen weeks since Shergar had been taken and almost as long since James Beag had first contacted me. The police were getting nowhere and – apart from the latest prospect of a reward through the insurers – I seemed to be getting nowhere.

I'd had my life threatened. I'd spent a lot of money. I could well be in serious danger following Drion's interview with the French press. I had material that I could turn into newspaper stories for which I'd already been offered a lot of money, but I'd been told I'd be shot if I made too much too public. Nor could I broadcast the stories. It was clear that my only prospects were to hang on, trying to persuade Beag to tell me more and more bits and pieces until some kind of coherent picture emerged, and to keep on pressing everyone to put up a bigger reward.

I still believed Shergar was alive and that he could be got back through Beag, but though I had some theories of my own already about what had actually happened on that night of 8 February, I had no actual proof.

Sifting through the theories made me realize just how little the police, the Government and the owners' syndicate knew. Everyone called it a kidnap, but was it even that? The one common element of kidnaps is a ransom demand. After the first two days, no calls or messages had apparently been received, although the rumours of photographs being sent and of confidence money being paid did suggest that eventually a full ransom might be negotiated.

One theory making the rounds, which could have tied in with my knowledge of the confidence money payments, was that ransom was being paid in instalments. The idea was that the owners wanted the horse back but didn't want to be seen to be bowing to blackmail, so they were paying up in dribs and drabs.

Equally, confidence money might have been paid by some of the syndicate members who wanted the horse kept alive so they could get it back, while others had refused to have any part in it. Those who weren't insured perhaps? Those who cared more for Shergar as a horse and didn't just think of him as an investment which could be recouped by an insurance claim?

A favourite theory was that it was a kidnap that had gone wrong. According to this version, the kidnappers had taken the horse with every intention of pursuing a ransom demand, but Shergar had been injured and had had to be destroyed. This theory accounted for the official 'silence' of the kidnappers after the first couple of days, but it didn't fit in at all with what Beag was saying, nor did it take into account the business of Flight 208 and the confidence money.

Then there were the non-kidnap theories – which said that Shergar had simply been stolen. Several possible reasons were put forward for the theft. Front runner – to use racing jargon – was that the horse had been stolen as an act of spite and vengeance against the Aga Khan, a man with many enemies, both spiritual and temporal.

There were a couple of weaknesses in this theory, though. The first was that the Aga Khan actually owned only fifteen per cent of the horse – though perhaps the gang didn't know that – and the second was that if the object was to embarrass and humiliate the Aga Khan, surely some kind of proof that Shergar was alive was necessary so the kidnappers could taunt him with the loss of his property?

I had felt for some time, however, that this theory was a very serious possibility. I had been picking up signs and hints that pointed in this direction, but I needed more proof before I could come out solidly in favour of the idea. I was convinced the kidnapping was the work of an international gang, but I didn't believe that foreign thieves could operate in County Kildare, or indeed within the Republic, without the help of one of the Irish illegal organizations.

Like Superintendent Murphy, though, I was pretty well satisfied that it wasn't a straight IRA or INLA job, if only because these organizations had never shrunk from claiming responsibility for indiscriminate bombings amd maimings, torture, executions, knee-cappings or bank robberies. Why should they be shy about claiming responsibility for kidnapping a stallion? In any event, my police sources were beginning to tell me more and more frequently that the IRA and INLA were telling them – the authorities – that they had *not* done the job.

A straight theft for gain was another possibility. Rumours were always starting in racing circles that Shergar was currently servicing mares in some Middle Eastern stud to help create a new breed of master-horses, or that his sperm was being sold all over the world for secret artificial insemination. The bloodstock authorities always said that this was nonsense because you couldn't fiddle the pedigree of a colt. Well, maybe, but as we say in Ireland, there's a couple of ways of skinning a rabbit!

The romantics all favoured this theory. Everyone secretly fancied the idea that some unknown yearling, with an undistinguished pedigree but maybe just a ghostly trace of a white blaze on his forehead, would come thundering round Tattenham Corner and steal the Derby 100 to 1. It's the kind of idea racing folk love, and I wouldn't want to rule it out – if only because, that way at least, Shergar would have a happy ending to his life.

Still, theories and mysteries were all very fine but my concern was to get Shergar back. I believed it was possible, but I was beginning to sense more and more that a major aspect of the whole situation was the way it was being mishandled by everyone concerned. Whether Shergar was recovered or not, my bet was that a blazing row was about to break out within the syndicate over the conduct of events since the kidnap.

After the interview with James Butcher I decided it would be as well to do some thorough checking into the exact ownership of Shergar. I knew many of the syndicate members already, indeed I'd spoken to quite a few of them in the course of the investigation, but I decided to get hold of a complete list – something that had been kept very quiet ever since Shergar disappeared.

When I did find out the breakdown of the thirty-four syndicate members, it made fascinating reading. It was like a mini 'Who's Who' of racing. Some of the names had already appeared several times in the press: Lord Derby, Robert Sangster, Captain Tim Rogers, Sir John Astor (who had given half his share to Lord Howard de Walden) and, of course the Aga Khan, but they were in equally distinguished company in the syndicate list.

One share, for example, had been bought by the Ardenode Stud, owned by the American millionaire J. R. Mullion. Another went to Paul Mellon, the American racehorse owner from Virginia, whose Glint of Gold won the Grand Prix de Paris in 1981 and finished second, ten lengths behind Shergar, in the English Derby at Epsom the same year. Four other American syndicate members were Bluefield Farm, in Nassau, Clayburn Farm, Lockridge Farms and Claude Leigh.

Another share belonged to the Moyglare Stud, owned by the owner and breeder, Walter Haefner (who, through involvement in other companies, had a say in a total of four shares). Two other members were Mailand Studs in Jersey, and the rubber magnate, Bertram Firestone, who also owned the Gilltown Stud at Kilcullen in County Kildare.

John Gaines of Lexington, Kentucky, and Sir Philip Oppenheimer, the diamond magnate – acting through his Hascombe and Valiant Stud – were also there. One share belonged to Juddmante Farms in Berkshire, owned by Khalid Abdullah, and another was divided between Ed Loader and a company called Brolan Investments – which had one share in all.

One very well known Irish name on the list was the Coolmore Stud at Fethard in County Tipperary, run by John Magnier, Vincent O'Brien's son-in-law and part of the operation run jointly by O'Brien and the pools-millionaire Robert Sangster.

Two more Arab owners also figured on the list: Mohammed Sheikh Bin Reshid and Maktoum al Maktoum. So did E.P. Taylor's Windfields Farms in Canada and the White Lodge Stud in Newmarket. Another share was listed for Sir Robert McAlpine, the building magnate, known in Ireland as the leader of McAlpines Fusiliers, the great army of Irish navvies and labourers who have built half of England's buildings and motorways.

The list continued with Paddy McGrath, a member of a great Irish racing family, and with a director of a newspaper chain, Waterford Crystal and the Irish Hospital Sweepstakes – Major John de Burgh of the Old Town Stud Farm. It also included Greek shipping millionaire, Stavros Niarchos, and the French owner, Jack Wertenheimer.

There were two companies on the syndicate list which caught

my attention particularly. One was Pantheon Limited, which is registered with a firm of accountants, Haughey and Boland of Amiens Street, Dublin, and which has as one of its directors Shergar's vet, Stan Cosgrove. The other was A.G.H. Herkimer Limited of Dame Street, Dublin, also run by Haughey and Boland, which had among its directors – until they resigned on 2 June 1981 – Stan Cosgrove, Ghislain Drion and Mary Charlton (who is Drion's secretary at Ballymany). Neither Cosgrove nor Drion had been mentioned as owners of Shergar and their actual shareholding in the companies was not stated. There was also a Swiss company called Dirgai, and a company called Moreton Bloodstock Management.

In the days following my talk with Butcher, I learned that two syndicate members– one in France and one in Britain – were very unhappy with the situation and were demanding to see the Aga Khan because they were convinced that nothing was happening.

Then, on Friday, 27 May, James Beag called again. He gave the signal on my home phone for me to go to Parliament Hill Fields, and as soon as he came on the line he wanted to know what was happening. He sounded eager, full of expectation, and I knew immediately that I would have to string him along a bit if I wasn't going to lose contact with him altogether. He was obviously desperate for his reward and he was counting on me. It seemed like a very good time to do some lying!

'Everything's going great,' I said. 'I've done as you said. I've seen Drion, Astor and Butcher. Astor is no good to us, but I've had a long talk with Butcher and the prospects there are looking bright.'

But Beag obviously wasn't interested in Butcher. I don't know what Ghislain Drion had done to Beag, but he'd certainly managed to upset him somewhere along the way.

'Tell me what the Frenchman said,' Beag replied savagely. 'Did you see him alone?'

I began to say that I had, but Beag interrupted straightaway. 'Was the SAS man hanging around?'

'Yes,' I admitted, 'he was there.'

I told Beag that I'd said to Drion I knew who Mike was.

'What did he say to that?' Beag asked.

'He was very disturbed and upset,' I said.

121

'Go on,' Beag said 'tell me about the froggie.'

'We met for about an hour,' I said. 'I told him what you wanted. I said that if they put up a reward of £100,000 or £150,000 they might get the person back. Drion is going to try.'

'Oh yeah,' Beag said bitterly. 'I'll believe that when I see it. He won't do anything.'

May the Virgin Mary forgive me, but I heard myself saying to Beag, 'Oh yes, he will. You have to trust someone. Trust Drion.'

I had about as much reason to trust Drion as I did to trust a bull in a field to say Mass, but it wasn't the moment for playing 'Truth' and 'Consequences'.

'What about the map?' Beag asked. 'Did you give him the map?'

'Yes.'

'What did he say? Did he shit himself?'

'No, he didn't,' I said, 'but he was shocked. He went white. We chatted about it. He asked where I got it. I said, "from this man".'

'Did he see the mark on it?'

'Yes,' I said, 'and I've got a lot of questions to ask you about that.'

'No,' Beag said. 'No questions.'

'Look,' I said, 'what does this bloody map have to do with the whole thing? Was that where the confidence money was handed over? Is that where the person is? Is that where he's buried?'

But all Beag replied was, 'Did Drion say he knew the place?'

'Yes,' I said angrily, 'he did say he knew the place.'

'Great,' Beag said. 'You did a great job.'

Then he hung up.

I was cross at getting nowhere again, but the feeling uppermost in my mind when I came out of the phone-box was relief. He obviously hadn't seen *The Irish Press* story, at least not yet, and I thought I'd managed to convince him that the situation wasn't lost. I wasn't so sure myself. Butcher seemed to be almost my last hope of raising a reward and he'd been completely non-committal, despite what I'd just told Beag.

For the next three days there were no developments at all, and I became more and more gloomy. It was beginning to look as though I was the only person who gave a damn whether Shergar lived or died. I went on thinking that way until the following Monday, 6 June, when another new figure came on the scene: Mr Terry Minahan, the Aga Khan's insurance broker.

The meeting was set up by James Butcher. I had had a call from him on the previous Tuesday saying that a talk with Minahan should be my next step. A date couldn't be fixed immediately. Wednesday, 1 June was Derby Day and I was fully occupied watching Lester Piggott winning his ninth Derby on Teenoso. Then Minahan was tied up, so we only got together eventually on the Monday. For the first time in more than two weeks, I began to feel some of the optimism I had lied to Beag about.

When I went to see Minahan at Dunster House in the City, I was expecting to meet a very high-powered insurance executive. Butcher had told me on the phone that Minahan was the Aga Khan's right-hand man, as far as insurance was concerned, and I wasn't ready for the very relaxed, low-sized man who greeted me. He was about five feet eight inches, with greyish sandy-coloured hair, and when I arrived he was working – jacket off, waistcoat loose. But what struck me most was the intelligence of his questions.

We quickly built up as good a relationship as you can hope for in the space of one meeting – even though it did go on for almost three hours, much longer than had been scheduled. I felt he was a worker, who knew his business and was willing to take a serious look at every option for getting Shergar back. It wasn't a quality I'd encountered much of lately and I did begin to feel that I might at last be getting somewhere.

Minahan began by making his own position clear. As the Aga Khan's broker, he had arranged about four million pounds' worth of cover on Shergar. This was to insure the Aga Khan's own shares and those shares being bought from him by instalments, and the cover was placed with two or three different groups of underwriters (including Butcher), but mostly at Lloyds. This made their policy the largest, and therefore the main one to be considered when discussions were going on. Any reports concerning the horse were fed to Minahan, but he said he had not necessarily been communicating everything to the brokers who were looking after the interests of the other shareholders because they were trying to keep the situation as confidential as possible and there had already been so many leaks and false reports in the press.

Once I had made my favourable assessment of Minahan, I gave him a full and complete account of what I had done since Beag's first call. I told him who I had seen and what their reaction had been and I was impressed by the fact that Minahan was already aware of a lot of what had been going on. At one point, Minahan said something which really caught my attention. When we were talking about Drion, Minahan said he had talked to him several times on insurance matters.

'But what one must remember is that most of my instructions on the insurance do not come from Ballymany at all, they come from Paris, from the Aga Khan.'

I had never had such strong confirmation before of what I had begun to suspect more and more – that Drion himself was merely a pawn and not the 'mover and shaker' he was claiming to be in his telexes to other syndicate members.

There was one point, though, that I felt Minahan had failed to understand, and that concerned the Aga Khan's failure to come to Ireland since the kidnap. Minahan felt it was understandable. The Aga Khan, he said, had only a fifteen per cent interest in the horse; it belonged now to a syndicate whose affairs were being managed through a syndicate committee which had met about a month previously in London and which the Aga Khan did not technically belong to.

But I think Minahan, like many other 'insiders', failed to understand the psychological effect of the Aga Khan's absence on the Irish people. The police and the syndicate desperately needed the co-operation of ordinary Irish men and women in the search for Shergar, but their attitude, as I well knew, was: 'If the Aga Khan can't even be bothered to come over to Ireland and show us he's concerned, why should we bother searching our fields and our barns and maybe risk trouble with the IRA and INLA?

However, despite this, Minahan and I were much closer in our views about a possible reward. Minahan began by saying that the insurers had made no move concerning rewards initially, because for the first ninety days after the disappearance they didn't technically come into the picture. After three months, however, the horse could be presumed lost and the claims become payable, and at this point Lloyds underwriters could consider an insurance reward.

But Minahan pointed out forcibly that some of the underwriters took the same view as some of the syndicate members – that if they gave in to a ransom demand, they would quickly find themselves facing similar crimes and similar ransom demands with other horses.

I objected equally strongly that my request on Beag's behalf was obviously a reward not a ransom. The figures alone showed it. Two million pounds might be called a ransom; £100,000 or £150,000 clearly could not – or at least, I didn't think so.

'Why,' I asked, 'have the insurers not considered putting up a reward of that kind of sum, say £100,000 or £150,000?'

'Probably because no one's asked them to,' was Minahan's reply.

At that, I left Minahan in no doubt that *I* was asking, and I wanted him to pass on the request to the underwriters concerned.

'I think it's possible,' Minahan said. 'Not definite, but possible. We need a group of insurers to do it. There will be people opposed to any sort of reward, but I think it's possible.'

I left Minahan's office with a distinct feeling that I might just have been able to pull the situation round at the very last moment. It seemed crazy to me that a group of Lloyds underwriters who cheerfully paid out huge rewards to recover stolen property after a bank raid, wouldn't see the sense of saving themselves several million pounds for what – in their terms – was a relatively paltry sum.

I was back in my old 'wait and see' position, but after my three-hour chat I had a great deal more confidence in Minahan than I had ever had in Drion.

The week ended, though, with an incident that reminded me that I was still very much out on a limb. It was a nasty little scare and I wouldn't want too many like it.

I was going back to the LBC studios in Gough Square after a routine sports assignment and when I got to the main entrance at about seven o'clock in the evening, the commissionaire, Bob, said, 'Did you meet your friend O.K.?'

'What friend?' I said, suspiciously.

'There was a fellow came looking for you. I told him you were out and he hung around the Square waiting for you. He stayed the best part of two hours. I thought he was still there. He was up to a little while ago, anyhow.'

'Jaysus,' I said, 'that's not the kind of news a friend should be after bringing me.'

From inside the studio, I had a quick look around the Square, then I spotted the figure, waiting in a doorway on the other side. He was carrying a small packet in his hand and the sight wasn't reassuring.

I thought for a few minutes about what to do. It had to be someone from Beag, I thought, if not Beag himself. I could hide in the building, or call the police, but that wouldn't solve anything. The man in the doorway hadn't actually done anything and he could always find me again. I decided I might as well go at it head on.

I walked across Gough Square and stepped towards the man. As I got closer I saw that he was dark-skinned, which didn't fit Beag very well, but I was so jumpy that I still couldn't get away from the idea that his first words were going to be, 'Hello, I'm James.'

The man stepped out of the doorway. 'Hello,' he said, 'I'm George. Are you Colin Turner?'

Instantly, it clicked. Putting the name George and the dark skin together, I realized that it was one of my listeners, a Sri Lankan I had never met but who was one of my greatest fans. He'd been writing to me for almost five years on and off, to thank me for the tips I'd given over the radio. George had won quite a lot of money following my programme, and there had been one especially big win. At the opening of the flat season, I had been sick with a cold and from home I called round a few trainer friends to get some tips for the Lincoln. I rather fancied Mighty Fly, which was being ridden by Steve Cauthen, but various trainers and other experts said they thought he wasn't ready. The way they were talking though, gave me the feeling that they were being over cautious, and I trusted my own instincts and made Mighty Fly my nap selection. It won at 14 to 1 and, along with a lot of my other listeners, George had won enough money to help pay for a trip he had been planning to Sri Lanka.

George greeted me with a broad grin.

126

'I just got back from Sri Lanka,' he said. 'It was great. I just came to thank you and bring you these.'

He handed me the packet, which contained some Ceylon Tea and some Sri Lankan newspapers – for me to see the racing form in George's homeland.

I have never been more grateful to see a fan!

Chapter 14

'Colin, I've asked the underwriters for authority to put up a reward of half a million pounds.'

Terry Minahan phoned the news to me on Thursday, 9 June, but he also left me in no doubt that he wouldn't necessarily get the authority.

'I can't give you anything definite,' he said. 'Really, some people say yes, some people say no. It's a question I suppose of a bit of democracy. They've got to debate it and one side will either win or lose, but I tend to think at the moment that there *will* be a reward put up.'

I said I was delighted with the news and I didn't think they would need to go as high as half a million pounds. Minahan agreed, and I suspect he had asked for that amount as a bargaining figure with the underwriters.

The other purpose of Minahan's call, though, was slightly more irritating. There was one more person he wanted me to see, a man called David Morgan. Minahan described Morgan as a 'sort of co-ordinator working for the insurance people'. He was an ex-Scotland Yard man, or something, but he was not strictly an insurance investigator, Minahan said.

'He's advising the insurers on what they ought to do, because the insurers are getting lots of leads and possible leads and they just don't know which are genuine and which are not.'

Minahan said that Morgan had met Superintendent Jimmy Murphy, and he mentioned at the same time that he, Minahan, had also met Murphy. (Though when I probed that a bit I discovered that he hadn't made a great impact, since Murphy had remembered him only as 'a man with glasses who came with another feller'.)

Reluctantly, I agreed I would see Morgan. Minahan said he

128

appreciated it, as the underwriters had more or less insisted on it when he had put to them my proposal for a reward. I decided there and then that I wouldn't tell Beag. I knew he would only get mad and hang up on me if he knew that yet another person had been added to the chain of people I was supposed to see.

During Minahan's call we also discussed the latest crop of newspaper rumours. The main one was a story in the *Sunday People* that some of the syndicate members (who had become known as the 'Syndicate Six') were planning to sue the Aga Khan for negligence over the stabling of Shergar. Minahan said he didn't believe it, but I wasn't so sure. I knew already just how much discontent there was within the syndicate. I thought the story was more likely to be based on a syndicate member saying what he'd *like* to do, rather than an actual intent, but there was no longer any doubt in my mind that real trouble was brewing among the owners of Shergar.

As it turned out, Minahan's call was just in time for me to be a bit more confident when Beag came on the line again. He called the next day, summoning me through the code to Parliament Hill Fields.

'So where's this good news you had for me?' he asked.

'It's coming, it's coming. It's definitely coming,' I said.

What the hell, I thought. I'd lied when there was even less prospect of a reward that there was now, why not go all the way?

'Look,' I said, 'Butcher put me in touch with another man.'

Beag's reaction was predictable, 'Oh Christ, not another one.'

'– but,' I went on enthusiastically, 'I've seen this new man. I've spent three hours with him. He completely understands what's going on now. He's talking to the people with money. Things will start to happen.'

Beag grunted. He sounded doubtful, but I was sure that some of my enthusiasm was getting across to him.

'And there's one thing *you've* got to understand,' I said. 'All this wheeling and dealing about money. I want nothing to do with it. When they're ready to do a deal or bargain or whatever, you have to arrange all that with them. The only thing I want out of this is the horse back alive.

'All the arguments about money will have to be direct between you and them,' I went on. 'I'm not standing in the

129

middle. They want it that way. I want it that way.'

I hesitated, then added one last piece of boat burning. 'By this time next week, the whole thing could be set up betwen you and them.'

'O.K., O.K. Right, right,' Beag said, as he hung up, and for the very first time he actually sounded happy.

When the call was over, I didn't have any regrets. I didn't want to lose contact with Beag and if the insurers backed off over the reward like everyone else, that was tough on Beag. I had done my best. I'd followed every one of his instructions. I'd chased all over the place on his behalf; the rest was now between them. Either the reward would come or it wouldn't. That was how I was beginning to think then, but I didn't realize that there were other, much bigger traps still lying in wait for me.

There was a brief interlude that week during which golf took over from racing as my main professional interest. On Monday, 13 June, I was presenting the Golden Fleece Pro-Am Golf Tournament at Wentworth in Surrey for Rediffusion TV and Video. It was an assignment I really enjoyed.

My job was to stand on the first tee, introduce the players, interview them, tell a few jokes and generally make the Tournament interesting for the thousands of people who were watching the drive-off on video in the refreshment tents and at other key points on the course.

Apart from the professional golfers, there were plenty of screen and television stars and many personalities from the world of racing. A point that was to become significant later – though I didn't realize it at the time – was that the 'racing' golfers included a number of Lloyds underwriters and others who were connected with the financial and insurance side of racing.

I interviewed a number of them that day – both on- and off-camera – and not a single word was spoken about Shergar. All the talk was of golf, and about Royal Ascot which was opening the next day. At the time, I wasn't really thinking about Shergar: one of the most important skills of my job is to be able to concentrate on the story in hand – but I was to remember bitterly my conversations with the 'horsey insurance people' I talked to that day.

When Ascot opened on Tuesday, 14 June, there was still no

130

firm word of the reward. It was a magnificent day's racing, and though there was some talk of Shergar, it was mostly about his past races.

The people who were really pressing me about the situation now were some of my colleagues in the press. They knew I was involved in the story – though, mercifully, they didn't know how deeply – and they spent a lot of time trying to pump me, fearing that I was going to spring a scoop on them. They got nothing out of me, not even a hint that I was following the story more closely than they were. I kept my worries about the reward to myself, fended off all their queries about Shergar with a joke or a crack, and concentrated on trying to pick winners, while enjoying the style and atmosphere of the Ascot scene.

The bombshell was to come on the second day. It was another great day's racing. The crowds were at their best, in brilliant sunshine, with not too much wind to worry the ladies in their Ascot hats. I put in a hard but very enjoyable day's work and in the late afternoon, when I'd wrapped up most of my broadcasts for the day, I was invited by a friend to join the trainer, Gavin Hunter, and his wife, for a 'going-home' drink in the car park.

In a way, that's typical of racing: they weren't actually celebrating anything in particular. Nobody in the party had won much money that day, but the champagne was flowing and there was lively racing talk and fun – a great crack – with a group that included top bloodstock agents, a TV executive and two delightful Americans, Des Scott, who owned a two-year-old called Hegemony, and a Los Angeles shipping magnate, Richard Corelli.

It was a fine Ascot gathering. We talked and chatted and traded tips for the following two days' racing, drank a glass or two of champagne and watched the elegant ladies parading past. However, Ascot is still very much a working week for me, and I broke off at about ten to seven in the evening, took leave of Gavin Hunter's party, and set off in my car along the motorway back to London.

By habit, I turned on the car radio. I usually listen to LBC while I'm driving and, anyway, it was time for the seven o'clock news. When the announcer began, I was only half listening – until I suddenly realized that I was listening to a dramatic news item about Shergar. The reader was saying that Lloyds had announced they were paying out seven million pounds worth of claims on Shergar as the statutory ninety-day period had elapsed. Then came the sting in the tail. Lloyds have also announced, the reader said, that they have been in contact with the kidnappers up to three weeks ago.

I heard the words clearly enough but I simply couldn't believe them. I was dumbstruck. People talk about being struck by lightning: it's never happened to me, but I suppose it must be the same kind of sensation. I was so shattered I wanted to get out of the car and be sick. They were naming me. I was the only person they could possibly be referring to. Right there on my own radio station – and presumably on every other radio and TV station in the country – Lloyds were exposing me and everything I'd told them in the strictest possible confidence.

I had kept my word with Beag despite a £10,000-offer for my story from Fleet Street. I'd tried to get the horse back, not to make a sensational story out of it. Now, I'd been as good as named and Beag could only think I was selling him out. I don't remember anything about the rest of the drive back. I went right across London in a kind of trance. I ended up at the studios in Gough Square safely, but it was a journey done completely on automatic pilot.

By the time I reached Gough Square, I was so angry I didn't know how to contain myself. As I drove into the Square I had a sudden urge to drive my Fuego straight through the plate glass window of LBC: I wanted to express my rage, my all-consuming fury that everything I'd been doing for months had just been destroyed by people I thought I could trust. I sat in the car, too angry to go inside. I went over everything that had happened and still I couldn't believe what I had just heard: I had seen a chance with Terry Minahan. I hadn't trusted many people during the whole affair, but I thought I could trust him. I had really believed he was a man who could do something. He'd led me to believe that we were almost there. I had only to see David Morgan, and wait for the expected approval of some of the other underwriters, and there might be, at last, a reward. Now they'd blown everything.

As I went over the situation, I also realized that I could be in very serious danger. Lloyds were saying they were dealing with the kidnappers – that meant me. They hadn't said they'd been

132

dealing with 'someone who'd been contacted by the kidnappers'. No. The news item was much more direct. They'd been dealing with the kidnappers. They had made me into a kidnapper. It wasn't going to be long before the full pack of Fleet Street hounds was on my neck. Someone who knew how close I'd been to the Shergar story would put two and two together.

Then there was Beag. He'd already threatened me with a bullet in the head if I stepped out of line. Drion had put me at risk with his *France Soir* story, but even that didn't compare with this. Beag was bound to think that I was deliberately sabotaging the whole operation, or that I was pretending to be a kidnapper and was going after a reward for myself. Either way, he would be coming after me.

I almost ran into the studio, and went straight to the newsroom. I asked the news intake tester, Vincent McGarry, to show me the 'tape' on the story – that's the raw material coming in on the wire services which is used to prepare news items.

He found it for me and it was all there – both on the Press Association and Extel 'tapes' – the two main domestic news agencies. The Lloyds statement had come through at ten minutes to six that afternoon. It was exactly as LBC had broadcast it. The ninety days were up, Lloyds were preparing to pay out seven million pounds and they had been in contact with the kidnappers up to three weeks ago.

No sooner was I in the news-room, than the duty editor said, 'Thank God you're here. Do a quick "voice piece" to update the story for later bulletins.'

'Yes,' I said, still completely in a dream, 'I will.'

I sat down at a desk and wrote an item for the thirty-to-forty-second recorded 'cart' – a cartridge of tape which could be slotted into the news bulletin in my own voice. I took the material and rejigged and reorganized it to present it in the style I would normally use. As I recorded it, I could feel myself trembling. When I got to the words 'Lloyds also stated that up to three weeks ago they were dealing with the kidnappers . . .' I fluffed, cocking up the 'cart' so badly that I had to do it again. I knew I was broadcasting about myself and I knew it was only a matter of time before other people found out, too.

I decided to get the hell out of the studio as quickly as possible. But first I called Superintendent Murphy at his home in

133

Newbridge. I wanted to explain my side of things before the police started coming to me. But I needn't have worried. He'd heard the story, too, and was very concerned for me.

'They're saying you're one of the kidnappers,' he said.

It had been Murphy's first thought – as it had been mine – when the news came over the air. Murphy was convinced I was being named and he warned me to be careful. I assured Murphy that I'd had nothing whatever to do with the story. I told him I'd played the situation exactly as I'd told him I would. I'd passed on Beag's requests, I'd briefed Minahan and I was waiting to see Morgan.

'Just be careful,' Murphy warned.

Even though I hurried, I still couldn't get out of the studios in time. There was more updating to be done and I had to watch the wires for further developments. Before long, Fleet Street started coming after me. First one, then another paper rang me. What did I know? What was happening? Was I involved in these negotiations Lloyds said had been going on? I managed to fend off everyone – at least for the moment – but I knew it couldn't last.

Eventually, I got to my flat and felt as though I was under siege. I was exhausted from the day's work at Ascot and the frantic rush at the studio, but I couldn't sleep. I was terrified. I was scared for my life and stayed awake most of the night imagining what was going to happen next. I could see bogeymen everywhere. I imagined a mob of journalists coming to get me. I could see them doorstepping my flat and the neighbours finding out why and coming to lynch me because I'd kidnapped Shergar.

I drank seven or eight cups of tea, tried to sleep, didn't manage it, and finally stayed up until about seven o'clock in the morning. I felt wretched. I was sick and scared and tired and then, when I thought I would finally get a couple of hours sleep, the phone calls started.

Ironically, the first one was from David Morgan. I'd been waiting to hear from him for three weeks, and now he was calling when it was already too late. Looking back, I have to smile at the way he began – as though nothing at all had happened.

'Colin Turner? . . . I've been talking to Terry Minahan on some things concerning Shergar . . . Is there any chance of a meeting to follow things up a little bit? . . . I think Terry explained that I had a role looking into various things on behalf of the insurers.'

I let him go through his apologies about how hard it had been to get hold of me since Monday, probably because of Ascot, then I brought him to the point.

'What about this crazy story from Lloyds last night?' I said. 'It's one of the craziest stories I've ever heard.'

Morgan said he thought it was just that; another crazy story, but he had been talking to Minahan about it.

'Well who released it from Lloyds?' I asked angrily.

'God knows,' was Morgan's reply.

So I told Morgan what I thought about the story. I said I was the only person who had been to see Lloyds three weeks ago, and I'd already had a couple of phone calls suggesting that it was me that was being talked about. I said I'd been to Butcher and Minahan with certain requests. Now the statement had come out saying that negotiations had broken off three weeks ago. I said that Butcher and Minahan had both led me to believe that there were no other negotiations in progress, so it sounded as though Lloyds was pointing the finger at me and saying I was negotiating for the kidnappers.

'I wasn't negotiating for the kidnappers,' I said. 'I was negotiating for someone else. Maybe one of them. I don't know if he is or not.'

Morgan repeated that neither he nor Minahan knew where the story had come from and he said firmly that he had absolutely no knowledge of any negotiations. Morgan also said that until I had mentioned it, it hadn't struck him that I was being named by the story. He said he'd assumed it was a piece of journalistic speculation and that when the press said 'a Lloyds spokesman' they meant that some pressmen had had a drink in a bar with someone in Lloyds who was involved on the fringes of the affair and didn't know what was going on anyway.

I wasn't going to let Morgan duck out like that. I told him that three people already – including the Superintendent in charge of the whole Shergar investigation – had assumed it was me. Others would start thinking likewise and I could hardly blame them.

'One of the things I was going to do this morning,' I said, 'was to demand to see Mr Minahan and Mr Butcher to know where their bloody story came from.'

Immediately, Morgan proposed a meeting with himself and Minahan. I agreed, but said I had to talk to my chief editor about the Lloyds story first.

Morgan suggested the afternoon, and said he would call me again once he had confirmed with Minahan. In fact, it was Minahan who called back, and I really went for him as soon as I picked up the receiver.

'How are you?' he asked.

'I hope you're much better than I am,' I said bitterly.

Minahan said he didn't think that was likely as he was inundated with calls about the Lloyds story.

'It's absolute bullshit, as you know. I don't know where the hell they got the story from.'

I said that I had a fair idea of at least one of the possible sources, since the previous night ITN had spoken to a Lloyds broker, Richard Milligan, who had confirmed the story. I said it was all the more strange since I'd talked to Milligan, along with a couple of other Lloyds people, at the Golden Fleece Pro-Am Golf Tournament at Wentworth and not one word had been said about Shergar.

'It's extraordinary, extraordinary,' Minahan repeated.

'So where the hell did this crazy bloody story come from?' I said furiously. 'You made me a guarantee when I came to see you that nothing would happen, nothing would break out until I see this man, Mr Morgan. I haven't seen Morgan. He rings me this morning and says he's been trying to get me, which is quite possible, but suddenly the story breaks last night and people are pointing the finger at me and saying Lloyds are going to claim you're the kidnapper.'

'I don't know what the hell it's all about,' Minahan said. 'Can we sit down together with Morgan at 2.30?'

Towards the end of the conversation, I was beginning to calm down a little but something Minahan said at the end really got me going again. He said he had been very annoyed when the story had broken but now he wasn't sure that it might not be beneficial.

'Maybe it's a damn good thing,' he said. 'Maybe the real people will think, "good heavens, they've been talking to

136

someone else by mistake, we'd better get in touch straight-away''.'

'No,' I said. 'Definitely not. The only thing this story could do for me is to put a bullet in the back of my head, as you and Butcher well know.'

We agreed to meet at 2.30, but before I could leave for the office, Beag rang the flat. He gave the signal for Parliament Hill Fields and I admit I was scared out of my wits. At the last call, I said everything would be settled within a week. Now, the whole thing was a total shambles. Apart from that, he couldn't have called at a worse time. I had an appointment with Ron Onions, my chief editor, which I was determined not to break, even for Beag. I owed Onions an explanation and I was going to need his help if Fleet Street started laying seige to me at LBC.

I rushed to Parliament Hill Fields, and by the time Beag came on the line it was already getting on towards the time I was supposed to see Onions. I didn't want to talk to Beag anyway; I was scared and I was angry. I wasn't in a fit state to handle myself properly and, for once, I was the one to cut short the call.

'I can't talk to you now,' I said. 'I just can't talk. I've got to go to the studio. You call me there.'

Beag started on about how he couldn't call the studio because I would record the call.

'There's no way I can record you when you come in on the public line,' I said. 'Just call me there. I've got to go.'

As I raced down to Gough Square, I wondered if I'd done the right thing. I'd been scared to talk but had I been too rough with him? In a crazy way, I'd come across very tough, just when I was the one who was scared for my life. Anyway, I'd done it, and I *did* have to see Ron Onions.

Onions saw me in his office at LBC, and I managed to slip through the news-room without getting involved in the Shergar queries that were buzzing around. Fortunately, Onions is very much a news-man and had been head of BBC TV news coverage in the United States before coming to LBC. It was much easier to level with him than with an executive who had come up through administration or finance.

I told him most of the story. I told him I was scared for my life and I wasn't free to broadcast what I knew about Beag because I'd likely end up with a bullet in the head. I gave him my personal assurance that I was not involved with the kidnappers in any way whatsoever, and I told him in no uncertain terms that I blamed Lloyds for the whole incredible mess.

Onions was very sympathetic. He was disappointed that I couldn't give LBC an inside exclusive, but he understood why and we left it that I would keep him briefed and that he would try to assist me in fending off queries from other news organizations.

I was relieved to have his support, but my calm didn't last long. I was barely out of his office and back in the news-room when Beag came on the line.

'So what the fuck has happened?' were practically his first words, and for once my glib Irish tongue couldn't come up with an easy answer.

'I don't know what's happened,' I said. 'It seems the gentlemen you put me in touch with have turned a little sour.'

I don't really know why, but I felt I had to explain myself to Beag. I'd got over the worst of my fear, but I still wanted him to know that I was not trying to pull a flanker and take the reward money for myself. Before I knew what was happening, I found myself almost pleading with Beag. I'd done everything I could to help him, I said.

'What they'd said at Lloyds was all wrong. Someone had leaked the wrong information.'

I kept saying, 'Do you believe me? Do you believe me?' I nearly cried on the phone.

I said I'd tell the whole story to a newspaper so he would know everything I'd done. I'd even write a book.

'Tell me, do you believe me?' I nearly screamed at him.

'Yes,' Beag said, 'I do.'

'I may have lied to you a bit,' I said. 'But I did think they were definitely going to come up with the goods. Drion stitched me up once with that story in the French papers, now Lloyds have done it with me.'

'I know all about the French story,' Beag said.

'You never told me you did,' I said, and I thought to myself, he really does believe me at last.

For the first time, I mentioned Terry Minahan by name. I said they might still put up the money.

Beag's answer was angry and bitter.

'They've completely fucked things up,' he said. 'They've screwed it up, the stupid bastards. They'll never see anything now. They're a parcel of fuckers for keeping us hanging on like this.'

'Maybe they don't believe you know everything,' I said. 'If the person was alive, they wanted proof and you didn't come up with anything. I could never explain it all to them.'

He didn't answer and I said again, 'I'll write a book about the whole thing. So everyone will know.'

Again, Beag didn't answer.

'Wait a few more days,' I said. 'Give Minahan time. The insurance people will put up some money.'

'They haven't got a fucking chance,' Beag said. 'We'll kill the fucking thing.'

And the line went dead.

Chapter 15

'CONTACT WITH SHERGAR'S KIDNAPPERS DENIED', *The Times* Shergar headline ran on Thursday, 17 June, over a story which began: 'Another hoax exposed yesterday in the extraordinary story of Shergar, the kidnapped Derby winner. This particular hoax was accidental, or so we are led to believe . . .'

The story quoted Lloyds as saying that a misunderstanding had arisen the previous day which resulted in the press and media carrying reports that agents for Lloyds had been communicating with the kidnappers until three weeks ago. *The Times* spoke of the underwriters 'holding a hastily convened meeting to question their press officer and find out how the story had emerged'. It said that underwriters, speaking at an impromptu press conference in a borrowed office in the City, confirmed Lloyds was prepared to pay out seven million pounds to the horse's owners who had insured against theft, adding that they would be liable for another one million pounds if it could be established that Shergar was dead.

One underwriter was quoted by *The Times* as saying that the report of negotiations 'could have done terrible damage to our reputation. If it were true, anyone could go and kidnap a horse and start negotiations with us.' And in the final paragraph, this is how the false report was explained according to *The Times*:

[The underwriter] insisted that there had been no communication of any kind since the last call in February on behalf of the presumed kidnappers ten days after Shergar's abduction in February; confusion had arisen because people had got in touch with Lloyds offering help and advice on Shergar's recovery.

The Daily Telegraph story was very similar and in some ways put the points even more strongly. The *Telegraph* quoted a Lloyds spokesman as saying:

> We have had no contact or communication with, or signals from, the kidnappers and we would not, under any circumstances deal with them. Lloyds insures scores of horses and other livestock and if it was thought that we had communications with the kidnappers, it could open the floodgates and jeopardize future insurance.

The Guardian carried virtually the same quote as the *Telegraph*, but with more detail on the Lloyds explanation. According to *The Guardian*:

> One underwriter said after the meeting 'Why the confusion has arisen is because we had genuine callers, people who want to recover the horse, and obviously we have to follow up those leads. We have passed those enquiries on to the Shergar syndicate and the Ballymany Stud.'

All of this floundering around by Lloyds took place after my meeting with Terry Minahan and David Morgan on the Wednesday afternoon, only an hour or so after Beag's call. The meeting was a bitter, angry affair. I'd calmed down a little since my first phone calls with Morgan and Minahan, but there was still a lot of 'effing and blinding' at the meeting and I left neither of them in any doubt that I blamed them for the colossal cock-up – which could well have cost the life of Shergar, not to mention my own.

Both men said – as they had on the phone – that they had absolutely no idea who had put out the Lloyds story. We discussed ITN's interview with Richard Milligan and they again said they knew nothing about that and would look into it. Neither then, nor later, was I ever told who was responsible. It was all blamed in a vague, general way on the 'Lloyds press office'.

Terry Minahan made me particularly angry at the meeting by trying to dismiss the announcement of recent contacts with the kidnappers as an unfortunate joke. He tried to laugh it off, as a stupid mistake which was completely coincidental and had nothing whatever to do with my relations with Lloyds.

I told him, with a good dose of Irish navvies' language, what I thought of that, and pointed out that it was my head the bullet might be going into, not his. If the situation was reversed, I said, I might be laughing and he might be worrying.

Gradually, the meeting cooled down and – mainly for David Morgan's benefit – we went over the whole Beag saga, right from his very first call to the LBC news-room. But, quite deliberately, I left out one call – the last one that had taken place just over an hour before.

I no longer trusted either of them. I didn't trust Lloyds, or Drion or the syndicate, and I felt it was up to Minahan and Morgan to show their good faith before I threw in Beag's latest threat to kill the horse because of the Lloyds cock-up.

Instead, I went at the problem of Shergar's death obliquely. I told them – truthfully – that at my meeting with Ron Onions he had said that if I didn't get a personal denial from Lloyds, Beag was going to think that no one cared about the horse any more and that they were going to pay up on the insurance and write the animal off.

What I didn't say, was that between my talk with Onions and my meeting with Morgan and Minahan, Beag had made just such a call. It was tempting to throw it in their faces, but I knew it was a time for caution.

When we had been through the whole sequence of events, Minahan came back to the eternal question: what does Beag want us to do?

'He wants to sell you information that will help you get the horse back alive,' I said. 'But it's too late. You've blown the whole thing now.'

Minahan protested that it wasn't necessarily blown. He said he would still get in touch with the other underwriters and try to raise the reward as he had promised.

'It's too late,' I said. 'You've cocked it up. You've blown it completely.'

But Minahan insisted that he would go on trying and he promised he would be in touch with me, within a day or so.

I was beginning to know the words of that particular song. I waited, but I didn't hold my breath, and I was right not to, because no call from Minahan ever came. I called him several times and eventually he admitted that there was no reward coming through. There was no agreement amongst the underwriters, some still opposed the reward. The situation was deadlocked.

That was still the position on Wednesday, 22 June, and the next day Beag made one more call.

It was short and bitter-sweet. He, too, seemed to have got over the violent anger he had felt after the Lloyds shambles, but there was no doubt about his resentment. He thanked me for what I'd tried to do for him and I said that maybe it wasn't over yet after all.

I suppose I was being over-friendly to him but I felt I was lucky to be alive. I wanted him off my back. I hadn't managed to get the horse back, but I didn't want to have to jump at shadows for months to come.

I said I'd been talking to Minahan again and that they were still trying to get a reward organized. I'd already told Minahan that if a reward was offered, I would try to set up a contact with Beag – though I refused to be the intermediary myself. Now, I tried to convince Beag not to write Lloyds off.

'They'll never come up with the money,' Beag said. 'They're a bunch of fools. They're afraid of their own shadows. They'll never see anything again.'

I pleaded with him not to damage the person. I said I would keep on trying. I still wanted to show Beag that I had played the game as he had asked me to, and I said again that I would write a book.

'Am I allowed to write a book?' I asked.

'I don't care what you do,' Beag answered.

I said a book could help, if only to show his side of the story, and I begged him again to allow a bit more time.

'Their time has run out,' he said.

'Tell me one or two things,' I said. 'If you're not one of the gang, who did the job in the first place?'

There was a pause, then Beag said, 'What's your second question?'

'If you're not in the gang,' I said, 'how do you know all these people you sent me to see and how do you know so much?'

Beag stayed completely silent. All I could hear was his

breathing on the line.

'Look, the way things stand,' I said, 'all I can call you in the book is a voice.'

There was another silence. Then he said, 'Just tell the truth about all those big powerful men with minds like mice.'

Then he ended the call, as abruptly as he'd begun the first that had started me off on the whole Shergar story, nineteen weeks before.

Whatever Minahan was promising, it now looked as though the story was going to go 'on to the back burner', as the Americans say. On one level, I was bitterly disappointed. I felt I'd failed to get the horse back, though I couldn't really blame myself. On another level, though, I was glad of an interlude. I knew I was lucky to come through with my skin intact and I had many other things to do that summer.

I didn't give up the investigation, I just let it take its place alongside my many other commitments. I live in Spain for a lot of the year, and for the next two months I spent a lot of time there, though I did make two trips to Ireland and kept very much in touch.

Early in July, I went to the Irish Embassy, this time to say goodbye to Dr Kennedy, who, sadly, was being posted to Rome. At the farewell party – attended, incidentally, by the Queen's press secretary, Michael Shea, who had been asked to convey Her Majesty's personal good wishes as a mark of esteem to Dr Kennedy – we had a quiet chat about Shergar.

I asked him why the Irish Government had done nothing. As a good diplomat, Dr Kennedy wouldn't comment, but I felt that he too found it strange.

For the next two months, fragments of information about the Shergar story came my way. But there was a big difference – the parrot, James Beag, was no longer sitting on my shoulder, muttering in my ear. I missed his calls, but I have to admit life was more restful without them, though I was still looking carefully into alleys and dark corners.

It wasn't until 17 September, while I was in Spain, that the story began to warm up again – and take on a new dimension.

I had a phone call from a European member of the syndicate who said there was to be a syndicate meeting in Paris on Saturday, 1 October – the day before the running of the Prix de l'Arc de Triomphe. My contact also mentioned that it was likely to be a stormy meeting as there were continuing signs of dissension among syndicate members.

I did some checking and found that he was right on target, there was trouble brewing. In fact, two letters were already circulating among members of the syndicate which were likely to cause everyone's views to come to a head at the Paris meeting.

I put more feelers out. Eventually, I discovered the contents of the letters and they really revived my interest in the story. Up to that point, I'd felt a bit beleaguered. I found that it was always me versus everyone else. I thought I was the only person who was really dissatisfied with what was happening. I seemed to be rowing with everyone. Now I had proof that, as I had long suspected, the syndicate members were rowing among themselves.

One of the letters was from a syndicate member, addressed to Michael O'Mahoney of McCann, Fitzgerald and Sutton in Dublin, the syndicate's solicitor. It objected strongly to the venue of the Paris meeting, on the grounds that it had apparently been arranged for the convenience of the Aga Khan and was *not* convenient for the majority of the shareholders, who lived in Britain and Ireland.

More significantly, the letter expressed deep dissatisfaction at the handling of the Shergar affair. It demanded a detailed report on the action that had been taken from the time of the abduction until the end of the contact with the kidnappers – if indeed the contact had ended. The letter complained about Drion's role, and the way the syndicate's committee had been working. It said Drion was not a shareholder; the other committee members were not readily available to members; and it spoke generally of the action taken as being 'too little too late'.

The letter also contained the explosive suggestion that the Aga Khan should be made to accept responsibility for the lack of adequate security at Ballymany and what it called 'the general neglect of the stud which was so apparent compared to other studs holding equally valuable horses'.

The other letter was to Drion from a syndicate member and was in similar vein, complaining bitterly about the state of the stud and also protesting about several aspects of the handling of insurance matters.

That second letter also contained sharp criticism of the Aga Khan, saying the writer thought he had treated the Shergar situation as a private affair, and not one that concerned equally other members of the owning syndicate.

With that kind of stage setting, it promised to be a fascinating meeting and, I must admit, I'd love to have been there. Not as a journalistic 'fly-on-the-wall', but with the right to speak, because quite frankly, I was beginning to feel I knew more about the Shergar situation than most, if not all, of the people present. Everyone knew his own little bit, but there seemed to be so little communication among them that I felt I had a much better grasp of the situation.

Anyway, I wasn't invited, but my ghost was – in the form of a few kindred spirits among the syndicate members. Fortunately, there were enough discontented members to brief me afterwards when it finally did take place, and I gathered that it was quite a meeting.

It took place in a Paris hotel and I learned that one member – one of the world's most prominent businessmen – had actually hidden in the toilet for more than half an hour, to cover his entrance and embarrassment at being seen attending.

If I'd been there, I'd have been on my feet within two minutes because I gathered that Ghislain Drion had reported there were no new developments in the search for Shergar. For whatever reason, he made no mention of James Beag or of my meeting with him or with Shergar's insurers.

One of the first items on the agenda was a request to the committee to pay out £57,000 for the cost of the investigation thus far. The 'technical adviser' concerned with the investigation was introduced, but not named. One or two members of the syndicate did ask for a bigger reward to be put up, but this was brushed aside, and the technical adviser, like Drion, made no mention of James Beag.

The syndicate members were told that despite all enquiries – which I learned later had included a trip by Morgan to the United States to see Wayne Murty, the Aga Khan's old enemy, who was an early suspect – they were still no further along the path of finding out what had happened to Shergar. There was, though, a certain amount of scapegoating going on. Drion told the meeting he thought the Irish Garda weren't up to much, and he thought that they probably had the wrong man leading the investigation.

Drion said he had established his lines of communication with the Government rather than the police and that the Irish Government had instructed him that no big ransom or reward should be offered.

Some syndicate members felt that, by saying this, Drion was trying to take the heat out of the situation, by making them think that the Government was directly involved when, in reality, it was hardly involved at all.

When this part of the meeting was reported to me, I was particularly curious about the comments on the Irish Government. Drion, it seemed, was saying that the Irish Government was ordering them not to pay rewards or ransoms, but I'd been picking up straws in the wind which suggested that the reverse might be true.

The technical adviser told the meeting that he felt secrecy in dealing with the press had been essential, and he said this had been endorsed by the Irish Prime Minister, Dr Garret FitzGerald. If the Aga Khan announced that he was pulling his bloodstock interests out of Ireland, other foreign owners would quickly follow suit, and an industry worth one hundred million pounds a year to Ireland would collapse – a point I had strongly emphasized back in April in my meeting with the Irish Ambassador.

The meeting had to content itself with a few pointed questions about the role of the Government in the investigation and the details of its contacts with the syndicate.

The meeting then discussed a report by Drion on the possibilities – apparently slim – of successfully suing Kildare County Council for negligence. There was also a row over insurance procedures. The meeting, I gathered, didn't exactly break up contentedly and I knew that none of these issues would go away.

There was also, I learned, an interesting tailpiece, which occurred the next day, during the running of the Prix de l'Arc de Triomphe at Longchamp. While All Along, a filly owned by his great rival, the art dealer Daniel Wildenstein, was winning the Arc, the Aga Khan was in his private box, telling several shareholders that *his* horse – Shergar – had, he suspected, been kidnapped and killed by the IRA.

147

Chapter 16

The effect on me of the Paris syndicate meeting was to sharpen my appetite for information almost unbearably. I always hate going back over old ground, but I decided it was time to see Monsieur Drion again and to throw my new information at him to see what his reaction would be.

I felt he owed me some explanations. I could have earned a small fortune in Fleet Street for the story of the syndicate row but I didn't broadcast it, or try to sell it to any newspapers. The price would have been high, but I felt it could have added up to thirty pieces of silver – for risking Shergar's death. I still believed the horse was alive, despite Beag's threats. I suppose in a way I had to believe it. That was what was making me press on with the investigation, but it wasn't just wishful thinking. I have a feeling about Shergar: I'm convinced he's going to turn up one of these days.

But before I could arrange an interview at Ballymany, there were other new developments. On Thursday, 6 October, *The Sporting Life* carried a story which referred to the 1 October syndicate meeting in Paris, saying that the idea of a bigger reward had been discussed. The story made the reward situation sound more promising than I knew it actually was. It was true the question had been raised, but it had been put aside, with no decision of any kind taken.

Still, *The Sporting Life* story was enough to bring a certain parrot flying back onto my shoulder. On Saturday the 8th I was at Wembley, doing the commentary on the Horse of the Year Show. I'd just got up from bed after three days with 'flu and I wasn't feeling particularly brilliant, but it was nice to be on my feet again and I always enjoy the show-jumping. In the middle of the evening I had a message from the studio: a man had tried two or three times to contact me, but wouldn't leave his name. I asked them to tell him, if he called back, that I'd be in the studios on the Sunday morning between 11.30 and 12.30 and again in the evening at six o'clock. The next morning, even though I was still feeling a bit ropey after the 'flu, I did make it to the studio on time at 11.30, and at ten past twelve, the switchboard put a call through to me.

'Hello,' the voice said. 'How are you?'

It was James Beag. He sounded calm, almost friendly. It was as though he was starting the calls new all over again.

'I'm fine,' I said. 'How are you?'

'Look,' he said, 'I won't keep you long. Just tell me what's happening. What's this in *The Sporting Life* about a new reward?'

I said it was possible there might be an increase, but I wasn't sure what the situation was.

Beag's next line had an awfully familiar ring.

'Can you go and see Drion? Ask him what's happening. Ask him again for an interview. Play it on your programme. Get him to do his own talking.'

I didn't tell Beag that I was already thinking of going to Ballymany. I thought I might as well make it sound like a favour to him, so I said, 'I'll see what I can do.'

'Talk to Moynahan as well,' Beag said, calling Minahan by the wrong name. 'Ask him how the money is.'

I said I would, and I was just going to ask Beag some more questions when I started getting interruptions around the sports desk. Several of my colleagues were bustling about and I could feel Beag getting uneasy again.

'O.K. I'll do that,' I said, 'and this time I'll contact you through the newspapers. I don't want the phone thing any more. I'll put an ad in the *Daily Mirror*. I'll write to JS [James Small] and I'll use racing jargon. I'll tell you if there's a lot of bread, and when it's all happening. Will you understand racing jargon?'

'Yes,' he said, 'I will,' and hung up.

I tried several times to get an appointment with Drion, and there were a couple of mix-ups with Drion flying to London while I was trying to contact him in Ireland, but eventually we set a meeting for Monday, 17 October at 11 o'clock.

I flew to Ireland on Saturday the 15th and broke with my normal routine. Instead of staying at one of my usual hotels, like the Gresham or the Burlington or Jury's, I checked in at a run-down little hotel on the South side of Dublin where none of my colleagues or friends would think of looking for me.

A number of people in Fleet Street were still keeping watch on me. They knew I was closer to the story than anyone, and they couldn't understand why I hadn't broadcast or published anything. Most of them assumed that I was just looking for a few more facts before launching a scoop – like waiting to draw a final card before going gin – and they wanted to be there, to ride on my back, if possible. If they saw me heading for Ballymany, the hue and cry would be well and truly raised.

Before seeing Drion again I also wanted another chat with Jimmy Murphy, and I arranged an appointment with him at the Garda headquarters in Naas for early on the Monday morning. I'd had several phone chats with him in the past weeks but there's nothing like a face to face meeting when you want to let your hair down, and Murphy and I had now established the kind of relationship where that was possible. On this occasion he gave me a really friendly welcome – it was almost as if he was greeting a member of his own family. He had separated me completely in his mind from the usual run of Fleet Street journalists who would, as he had learned to his cost, write any kind of rubbish to keep their editors happy.

I told Murphy I was on my way to see Drion and gave him a fairly detailed run down on what had happened at the 1 October owners syndicate meeting in Paris. I held back some things, just as I'm sure he held back a number of important matters from me, but, on the whole, we were as frank with each other as ever, or as frank as is possible between a policeman and a journalist.

I discovered that we were now in general agreement on several points, including that the IRA were involved only marginally. He had come round to my view that the kidnap was the work of an international gang, with the IRA or the INLA providing local knowledge and experience. I told him that the Aga Khan had been saying in Paris that the IRA might have kidnapped and killed Shergar. Murphy was not impressed. He felt that the Aga Khan had stayed so far out of things that his theories didn't really carry much weight.

We also talked briefly about the groom, Jimmy Fitzgerald, who had almost become the forgotten man of the Shergar affair. Since the kidnap he hadn't said anything to anyone and was still, by all accounts, a very shaken man. In Superintendent Murphy's own words, Fitzgerald had 'looked hell in the face' that night, and he recalled that when he had questioned him the next morning, he had had to put his questions with great gentleness and caution as he had been afraid Fitzgerald might have a heart attack.

We went back over the story together and then talked about Waterford again. Murphy said he had turned up nothing significant about the two men I had mentioned, so I reminded him of a very recent case in which arms bound for Northern Ireland, hidden in crates marked 'European Electronics', had been seized in the French port of Le Havre, and Murphy promised to investigate further.

All in all, it was a reassuring interview. It didn't advance the situation particularly, but it was satisfying to know that none of my conclusions was seriously at odds with those of the man in charge of the police side of things. With that extra touch of confidence, I headed for Ballymany and my rematch with Monsieur Ghislain Drion.

The first thing I noticed as I entered the Stud was that it looked a bit cleaner than it had on my first visit. I wondered if some of the criticism being heard around the syndicate was washing back to Drion, and yet, despite the improvement, I have to say that for a stud in this league, it did leave a lot to be desired. Over the years I've visited many stud farms in Ireland, Britain and the United States, and by top-class standards Ballymany was what I would call dirty.

I drove slowly up the long avenue and, when I reached the office, I was greeted by the same low-sized French clerk in the oddly-shaped wire-framed glasses who had been there on my previous visit. He asked me to wait, but as soon as he had announced me, Drion himself came out of his office and invited me to step in. We shook hands and he said it was nice to see me – which I doubted, but politeness is a wonderful thing. A woman secretary offered me tea and I sat down and made myself comfortable.

The office definitely *had* changed. If the Stud outside had been cleared up a bit, the office had been tidied up a lot since I was last there. The whole place looked bright and shining, and even though there were still piles of papers on Drion's desk, everything looked very orderly and businesslike.

I was well-prepared and ready for the interview, but before we got down to the conversation, we had one very big problem to overcome: the question of tape-recorders. While Drion was talking to his secretary about something before arranging for us not to be disturbed, I had my 'executive note-taker', a small micro-tape-recorder, in my hand and I pressed the 'play' button to check that it was working properly. At that precise moment Drion came back into the room, and when he heard the click of the button, he reacted as though I'd fired a shotgun at him!

'What is that sound?' he almost shouted.

I explained that it was my tape-recorder, one I used to keep notes, record appointments and remind myself of what had been said during conversations. As Drion listened, I thought he was going to have a fit.

'You cannot use that. You cannot use that,' he said.

I said it wasn't an ordinary tape-recorder; it was just for taking notes and reminding myself of things.

Drion took it from my hand as though it was a piece of plastic explosive. He held it out and looked at it carefully, then turned it over, held it up, and examined it from every angle. I said I would like to use it to make some notes of our conversation.

'No. No. You cannot use this thing here,' Drion said.

'Look,' I said, 'it's only for office use. You can't use this kind of recording on radio. Did you think I was going to record you?'

'No. I just don't like them.'

He was really uptight and I decided that, if he was going to act like an old woman, I would do my best to reassure him.

'All right,' I said. 'Why don't you hold on to it during our discussions?'

Drion did so, but you would have thought it was going to explode any minute. All through the interview he kept looking at it, and from time to time he would touch it, or turn it round on the table top.

Eventually, we got under way and Drion began by asking if I had any news for him.

'I came here because I want news from you,' I said. 'But can

152

we go back to my last visit? I am still waiting for you to call me. The last time I was here, you promised you would call. You gave me your assurance.'

Drion hesitated and looked ill at ease. 'A lot of things have happened since then,' he said. 'And I have been very busy. Tell me now what you want to know.'

'O.K.,' I said. 'Let's start with the map. Tell me first what you did with the map I gave you when I was last here.'

Drion thought for a moment, then he said, 'Oh yes, I gave it to the police.'

'You mean Superintendent Jimmy Murphy?'

'Yes. I gave it to Murphy.'

'Are you sure?' I asked.

'Yes.'

'No,' I said. 'You didn't. Murphy has seen the map. But he got it from me. He didn't get it from you. Who did you give it to?'

'Well,' Drion said, 'I passed it on. Why do you ask?'

'Because who ever you gave it to, or whatever you did with it, you nearly got me killed.'

'Oh no,' Drion said. 'That cannot be so.'

'Oh yes, it is so,' I said. 'Who did you give it to?'

Drion paused. 'Maybe I gave it to someone in a high place,' he said finally. 'But I know the police got it.'

'You mean the French police got it?'

'It could be,' Drion said.

'Now,' I said, 'tell me about the newspaper story in *France Soir*. Four days after I walked out of this office, someone tried to get me killed and, to be honest about it, Monsieur Drion, it was you!'

'How?'

'This French newspaper ran a story saying that the Aga Khan had come under threat of death from the kidnappers, as they were looking for a big ransom payment. You were quoted in the story and it said the Irish police had secretly gone to France after getting certain information. One, this upset the Irish police, who say they didn't make any secret trip. Two, it upset the Irish Government. And three, it nearly got me killed. The Irish Ambassador himself was the first one to ring me and tell me about the story and he said ''someone is trying to get you into big trouble".'

'But who would cause you this trouble?' Drion asked.

'The man on the phone and his friends, if he thought I was double-crossing them. That's who,' I said.

Drion sat still for a moment, not answering, then he said slowly. 'I do not know about this. I did not try to get anyone killed.'

There was no point in arguing any futher. I'd made my point and all that was in the past. My concern was to try and get something moving now.

'Tell me this,' I said. 'Why hasn't the syndicate put up any reward money?'

Drion simply could not answer. He muttered one or two things but he couldn't even think up a plausible excuse. He just did not have an answer.

I reminded him that the last time we had got on to this subject, our meeting hadn't exactly ended in a friendly manner and I hoped it wasn't going to go that way again.

Drion still didn't answer, so I pressed him on a different tack.

'At this stage, Monsieur Drion,' I said, 'do you believe Shergar is alive?'

'What do you think?' Drion replied, after pausing for a moment.

'I believe he's alive,' I said.

'That's very good,' Drion said, with a half smile. 'At least we agree on one thing.'

But I wasn't going to let that pass so easily.

'Monsieur Drion, you shock me,' I said. 'The last time I was sitting in this office, you told me Shergar was dead. What changed your mind?'

Drion hummed and hawed, but didn't answer directly.

'The thing is,' I went on, 'if you think Shergar is alive, why is the Aga Khan going round telling other members of the syndicate that the IRA killed the horse?'

Drion sounded surprised. 'That's not what he's saying,' he said.

'Yes he is,' I said. 'He definitely is. I've been told by four or five members of the syndicate that this is what the Aga Khan has been telling them.'

I had a sudden thought and decided to try a flyer.

154

'I know why you think that Shergar's alive,' I said. 'You've seen a new photo.'

Drion paused. 'No. I have seen no photo.'

The denial was direct enough, but Drion seemed puzzled and disturbed by my remark. I didn't know myself whether there was a photograph. The rumour that there was one had been circulating again, and Beag had hinted that new information had been passed to Ballymany. I put them together to see if the idea had any effect on Drion.

'Who told you about a new photograph?' Drion asked.

'The man on the phone told me,' I lied. 'If you haven't seen the photo, you know about it.'

Drion again denied that he had seen any photograph. He tried hard to change the subject, but when I wouldn't leave it alone, he said finally, 'It may have gone to the Paris office.'

'Isn't it true,' I asked, 'that a helluva lot is done through Paris without coming through here? Why don't you do something at this end?'

'What do you want me to do?'

We were back on the same old roundabout, and I wasn't enjoying the ride very much.

'Monsieur Drion,' I said. 'The syndicate met in Paris on 1 October. After that meeting, there was a suggestion in the press that a new reward offer might be made. The man on the phone sent me over to see you to find out if it was true. I've told you many times what he always says: "Get Drion to do his own dealing." He said to me this time exactly what he said last time: "Go and see Drion. Record an interview with him. Let him say if there *is* a reward." '

'I can't do that,' Drion said.

'Monsieur Drion,' I said. 'Is the man on the phone right? Have you got someone handling this whole thing for you?'

Drion didn't answer immediately, but when he did, it was to make his first full admission that Beag had in fact been right all along. Drion admitted that after taking the first two or three calls made to Ballymany after the kidnap, he had passed the whole operation on to other people. He hadn't taken calls, or called back when messages were left for him. He had – as Beag had so often put it – let others do his dealing for him.

'It's certainly what happened to me,' I said. 'Whenever I

155

called Ballymany I was always shunted on to someone else. When I tried to talk to you at the beginning I never could.'

With Drion now much more ready to confess some of the things he had held back previously, I encouraged him to go back over the whole situation, right from the disappearance of the horse on 8 February. In particular, I quizzed him closely about the delay there had been in informing the police. For the first time, Drion gave me a completely straightforward answer.

'I couldn't find the Aga Khan,' he said simply. 'It took me almost three hours. You know what the Irish telephone system is like. He wasn't at his home in Sardinia and he wasn't in Paris. Eventually, I tracked him down in St Moritz, in Switzerland. That was what took the time.'

Drion seemed to find the delay justified. He obviously found it unthinkable to act without direct instructions from the Aga Khan.

'You realize, don't you,' I said, 'that all that time you were pissing about, Shergar was getting further and further away? God forbid that anything like this should happen again, but if it does, you've got to have faith in someone. You have to act on your own. This man on the phone in London, he thinks you're a real wanker.'

It was a mistake to say it. I didn't mind calling him the name – I happen to agree with Beag's judgement anyway. But Drion didn't understand the word.

'Tell me, Monsieur Turner,' he said, in his strong French accent, 'what is a "wanker"?'

It took me three minutes to explain the word, and by the time I'd got the message across, the atmosphere wasn't too brilliant and the conversational flow was what you might call broken. Drion wanted to break the meeting off but I certainly wasn't having that. I didn't care whether Drion was offended or not. I wanted to talk about the Paris syndicate meeting.

'What about the investigation that is supposed to have been done?' I asked.

'What do you mean?'

'As I understand it,' I said, 'a bill for £57,000 was put on the table at the Paris meeting by the Aga Khan for an investigation done by your technical adviser.'

Drion looked really shocked that I knew this, and when I went

156

further and began to give details, he seemed completely stunned.

'Isn't it true that David Morgan is one of your technical advisers? Isn't it true that he went to see Wayne Murty in America because Murty was the number one suspect? And isn't it true that he got nowhere, and that was what most of the investigation consisted of?'

Drion wouldn't answer, so I said, 'You know the Aga Khan has other enemies besides Wayne Murty. What about Colonel Gaddafi, the Libyan leader, for example? He hates the Aga Khan and has talked about pulling this kind of coup. What about him?'

Again Drion refused to comment, but I could see that he was really disturbed by this speculation. I think he had got so used to handing out the feeble 'official Ballymany' line that he was really ill at ease when confronted with having to make decisions about real possibilities. Plenty of people – myself included – believed that Colonel Gaddafi was a very serious suspect. He had the necessary ruthlessness and the necessary resources: his people had carried out terrorist acts in various parts of the world and he had plenty of links with the IRA. Irish terrorists had been trained in his camps in Libya alongside PLO fighters and left-wing terrorists from half a dozen countries. He did hate the Aga Khan enough. But Drion wasn't willing to discuss it even as a possibility.

'Who do you think did it?' he asked me at one point.

'You're hoping I'll say the IRA,' I replied. 'Well it wasn't a straight IRA job. They may well have helped. But the gang was international. The Irish police are being told by the IRA that it wasn't one of their jobs. I think you ought to start looking towards the Middle East a bit more.'

During the conversation, Drion pointed to travel stickers on the leather bag lying at my feet beside the big tape-recorder.

'I see you go to the Middle East,' he said.

'Yes,' I said. 'I'll go anywhere there is sun. That's why I live in Spain for most of the year.'

'You live in Spain?' Drion asked, very surprised.

'Yes.'

'Some members of the syndicate live in Spain too for some of the time,' he said.

157

I wasn't being drawn down that line! Drion was about to start fishing to find out who my sources were, and I quickly put the conversation on to a different path.

'Monsieur Drion,' I said, 'apart from the trip to see Wayne Murty, the investigators haven't turned up many suspects, have they? Isn't it true that some members of the syndicate are refusing to pay their share of the £57,000, the investigation cost, until they have more details of what's been going on?'

'How do you know that?' Drion said sharply.

'I know a lot of things,' I said. 'You must have realized that by now.'

'You should speak to David Morgan,' Drion said. 'Yes, you should definitely speak to him.'

'Yes,' I said, 'I plan to. But in the meantime, what are *you* going to do?'

'What do you want me to do?'

'I want you to tell me in your own words what the whole situation is now. And especially about any reward.'

Drion looked anxious; it was the look he always got when I tried to pin him down.

'As I told you last time,' I said, 'I'll give it all to the media. BBC, ITV – everyone.'

'I will need to get permission,' he said nervously.

'Fine,' I said. 'Why don't you call the Aga Khan right now? I can wait.'

'No, I cannot do that,' Drion said. 'But I think you have a good idea. If we increase the reward money, I will ask the committee if I can do this interview with you. I'm sure they will agree.'

It was then that I decided there was no point in carrying on the conversation. Drion simply didn't have spine enough to act on his own. We were going round in the same old circles and – knowing Drion as I had come to know him – we were going to go on doing so.

I brought the conversation quickly to a close and Drion was obviously very relieved that I was giving up. We said our goodbyes, and as I drove away from the office down through the rolling slopes of the stud farm, I couldn't help feeling sorry for him. He was ineffectual – Beag had found the right word to describe him – but the Aga Khan's high-handed attitude was obviously at the root of the problem.

Before I left the area I had a few more calls to make. I had been told of a man I should contact who had once worked at both Ballymany and the Aga Khan's other Irish stud, Sheshoon. Apparently he had some information to pass on, and he could also help me to identify the photographs of some of the people going in and out of Ballymany, which I had arranged to have taken by a local photographer.

The meeting had to be kept very quiet, so after seeing Drion and making one or two calls to other members of the syndicate, I had to wait around until it got dark. It had been raining from early afternoon, but by nightfall it was really bucketing down; the roads and fields were completely sodden, and visibility both by car and on foot was down to a few yards.

My original directions for finding the man turned out to be wrong, and I ended up right inside the Curragh Army Camp. I don't know how it's possible to get inside a military establishment in Ireland that easily, but I managed it somehow, and I only realized it when I passed the sentries on duty as I was finding my way *out!*

I obviously needed new directions, so I drove around until I found the Rising Sun public house, right in the middle of the Curragh. The problem was that I couldn't ask outright for the man I wanted to see. If I mentioned his name in the pub, word of my interest in him would be round the area like wildfire. So I had to ask for directions to somewhere I thought was fairly near the house I actually wanted. In Ireland, if you ask a Mickey Mouse question, you get a Mickey Mouse answer. But I hadn't really any choice. They say that people in the country districts of Ireland can hear the grass growing, and if I gave the slightest clue to my real destination they would pick it up.

Finally, these were the directions I got – and I suppose they were all I deserved!

'Go down the road for about four miles until you pass a bush on the left-hand side. Don't take the first turn, but the second on the right. Now if it wasn't the night that is in it, at that second turn a fierce dog that belongs to the woman who lives at the cottage will come bounding out. He comes out and barks at everything but he won't tonight because it's raining cats and dogs out there. So it's not the first turn by the bush, it's the

159

second turning. Now if you go beyond that second turning and take the third turn, then you'll be lost and you'd better turn back!'

Fortunately, my personal angel was on my side, and I found the right turning. I drove my car down a narrow country road for about two miles. I had been told I mustn't park anywhere near the house, and if possible mustn't be seen. So I hid the car as best I could and walked across a rain-sodden field, climbed a few hedges, got covered in cow dung and fell into a drain which was already overflowing with rainwater. By the time I eventually reached the front door of my contact's house, my black leather town shoes were a complete write-off and my slacks, jacket and topcoat were all ready for the nearest dry-cleaners – with me along with them.

My contact came to the door with a small baby in his arms. He had been left in sole charge, and I think the sight of me after my scramble through the fields and ditches scared them both a bit!

We had an interesting chat about the IRA and he felt, as my other contacts did, that they were not the main people involved in the kidnapping. The baby stayed silent through most of our meeting, but it was very odd to be talking about the IRA and the INLA while he searched around for a dummy to keep the baby quiet, and while I tried to work out ways not to drip mud and water all over the furniture and the carpet.

His information was very interesting, though it provided nothing really new, but his help with the photographs was invaluable. He knew everyone and he stood, with the baby at his shoulder, looking at each one and giving me the names of all the people, together with a little bit of local gossip about each of them.

When he had finished, I stroked the baby's head, put a five-pound note in his rompers and said, 'There, you buy your Daddy a drink with that.'

Then I was shown out and I struggled back across the fields. I managed to avoid the drain this time, but I had to clamber up a bank and, when I did finally reach the comfort of my car, I was barely fit to sit in a lorry taking Irish navvies to and from work, let alone in a half-decent saloon car!

After leaving the man to look after his baby, I had one more call to make. The description of it must necessarily be brief as it was to a man with connections to Sinn Fein. I had been told in advance that he would be willing to answer one or two questions but only with a 'yes' or 'no' answer and without giving details. I put to him the question I was putting to most of my best contacts.

'Did the IRA do this job alone?'

His answer was, 'No'.

I asked then, 'Was the IRA involved?'

This time he answered 'yes', but again gave no details.

Finally I said, 'Who knows about this IRA involvement? Do the police know? Does the government?'

His answer was a firm 'I don't know', and the conversation was brought to an end.

It gave me more to think about on my way back to England the next day, but at least this time I wasn't going to hold my breath waiting for a call from Monsieur Drion. Ironically, though he didn't call, I saw him again much sooner than I had expected to.

On the next day, Wednesday, 19 October, I had to attend Sandown Park in my capacity as a sports commentator for IRN and LBC, to report the international challenge match between jockeys from the United States and the United Kingdom. The first of the three challenge races was won by the Aga Khan's horse, Nassipour, ridden by the American jockey Chris McCarron, but it was the fifth race that was to bring me and Drion together again.

Just a few minutes before the start of the race Drion and his wife, accompanied by the Aga Khan and the Begum Aga Khan, jetted into Sandown Park to see a half-brother of Shergar's, Shernazar, run. They saw the young two-year-old put up a very good performance to finish second behind Test of Time. After the race, the Aga Khan's party came back to the unsaddling enclosure to welcome back their colt and to talk to their trainer, Michael Stoute.

They were ignored by most of the Fleet Street racing press who would normally have crowded into the unsaddling enclosure to ask for comments and information about future plans. So this gave me the opportunity to approach the party and have a word with Drion.

He was as surprised to see me as I was to see him. I welcomed him to Sandown Park. I said I thought the colt had run very well and they must be very pleased with the performance of this nice-looking horse. Drion said yes, they were all very pleased, and they were more pleased that the jockey had not given the horse a hard race. At that point, we seemed to have run out of conversation about Shernazar and Drion said to me, 'Have you got any news for me?'

I said, 'No, I was expecting some from you. I only arrived back from Ireland last night. I was hoping that you would have talked to the committee by now and set up that interview for me.'

I'll leave you to guess what his answer was. But as a hint I'll tell you that it began with the words, 'Yes, yes, Monsieur Turner, we will let you know . . .'.

Chapter 17

It was obvious now that I was going to have to give up on Monsieur Drion, but I was determined not to give up altogether. Clearly the insurers were now my best bet, and I decided to go back urgently to Terry Minahan. We made an appointment for Friday, 21 October and met, once again, in his office in the City. We were both very cautious. I knew I needed Minahan, but he had to prove to me that I could trust him, so we chatted and talked until he started to give me a few pieces of information which showed me he was willing to take me into his confidence.

He told me, for example, that there had been no separate insurance investigation. He said that David Morgan had been working for the underwriting syndicate as well as for the Aga Khan and the owning syndicate.

Then Minahan made some other comments which made me wonder even more if the underwriters were looking after their interests as well as they might. Minahan told me that the underwriters had never had a meeting with Drion and neither had the brokers.

I said: 'Do you really think it's wise to put everything in the hands of Ghislain Drion, a man who seems to be totally incapable of making a decision, even if his own life depends on it?'

Minahan had no answer for that, and I sensed that he pretty much agreed with me, but wasn't free to say so.

In the course of the conversation, I mentioned that I'd been told that some members of the syndicate were considering taking action against the Aga Khan because of the deplorable state of the Ballymany Stud and the amazing lack of security. I added that one syndicate member had complained to me that there was

163

no videotape in the camera at Shergar's barn. I wasn't sure myself whether it was the kind of camera which was meant to have tape in it, or whether it was supposed to be linked directly to a monitoring screen in another part of the Stud. But it's always useful to have sticks to beat people like Minahan with, so I put the member's complaint to him to get a reaction.

Minahan said he didn't think it mattered either way.

So I asked him how the kidnappers knew the camera was useless. He didn't answer.

'If I were a kidnapper,' I said, 'I wouldn't waste time worrying whether there was a film in the camera, or a tape, I'd shoot the thing off the wall.'

'Are you suggesting it was an inside job?' he asked. 'You mean the kidnappers knew the camera wasn't a threat because it wasn't working?'

'Yes,' I said. 'They must have had some inside information.'

Minahan grinned. He just nodded his head, and I didn't tell him that the staff at Ballymany felt the camera was useless. I could see that there were limits to the extent he was prepared to defend the state of Ballymany.

Minahan did admit, though, that the Aga Khan had brought in his own security people after the kidnap and that they included Mike, the ex-SAS man, but he said their main purpose had been to stop the press coming in and generally to protect Drion, who was at a big disadvantage because of his French accent and limited command of English. Minahan said he was convinced himself that most of the people involved believed the Aga Khan was really pulling all the strings and that Drion was only a front man, whose main purpose was to stand in the way while the shit was being thrown so that none of it stuck to the Aga Khan.

Once some kind of mutual confidence was re-established between us, I came straight to the point of the conversation: I said I still wanted a reward. I said I'd been to see Drion and James Beag had been back in touch with me, wanting to know about the reward money that had been mentioned in the article in *The Sporting Life*.

In that great journalist's and diplomat's phrase, Minahan was 'cautiously optimistic'. He said a reward would be announced. He didn't know yet the exact amount and he didn't know whether it would be put up entirely by the insurers or whether there might also be some syndicate money involved. I judged from Minahan's tone that he really did believe that there was a reward in the making, but I'd been bitten too many times to be certain.

I said I would like to talk to David Morgan because there were a number of things I could say only to him. Minahan didn't like this very much. He kept saying, 'But you can talk to me. There is no need to deal with Morgan.'

When I insisted, Minahan said that Morgan was away in the Middle East, but he promised to try to arrange a meeting as soon as he was back in the country. I told Minahan that Drion had also insisted that I see Morgan.

We parted on an optimistic note, with Minahan's assurance that a reward was now finally in the pipeline. I was prepared to believe him, but I made a few phone calls over the week-end just to cross-check, and the results weren't very encouraging.

I spoke to a couple of the syndicate members who told me that they had not been asked to put up any contribution to reward money and they had not heard of any other syndicate members who had. That made me a bit dubious again about Minahan's statement, since he had said there could well be syndicate people involved as well as underwriters.

I was itching to know so badly, that on the Monday morning, 24 October, I rang Minahan and asked for an urgent meeting. I wanted to be positive, sure and certain that I wasn't going to be double-crossed again. Getting a reward put up had been my goal right from the very beginning and it looked as though it was within my grasp. I didn't want any last minute skulduggery on the home straight.

When I saw him Minahan asked me politely why I had come back so quickly. I gave him a straight answer. I said I'd come back for the simple reason that I had spoken to some members of the syndicate over the week-end and that they hadn't been asked for any money to go towards a reward. More than that, the people I had talked to had had conversations with other syndicate members and there had been absolutely no talk of a reward. One or two knew of money demands, but didn't know who they were from.

'So you see, Mr Minahan,' I said, 'you'll have to give me better proof that a reward does exist, because otherwise people just aren't going to believe me when I tell them.'

165

'Honest to God, Colin, it exists,' Minahan said. 'I can show it to you. Don't you believe me?'

'No,' I said. 'Show it to me.'

Finally, Minahan gave in. He went to a cabinet at the right-hand side of his office, opened it and took a document out of a file. It was a large double-foolscap-sized sheet of paper which he opened out in front of me for me to examine.

On the top left-hand side was the name 'Leslie and Godwin' and close by, in a small box, the notation LFN 727. In the centre was the title of the document 'SHERGAR REWARD' and below, set out in typescript, were the full details.

It said that a reward of £250,000 would be offered for the recovery of Shergar, dead or alive, and for information leading to the arrest or conviction of one member of the gang. The extreme right-hand side of the document was divided up into about forty squares and in each one was the signature of an underwriter who had agreed to the reward.

It was everything I had hoped for. This was my 'Olympic Gold Medal' – the prize I had been struggling for throughout nearly nine months. It even had the important proviso that only one member of the gang need be convicted. Beag had dismissed completely the idea of a reward when it stood at £60,000 for information leading to conviction of the gang, but 'one member' was different and the stakes were higher. It gave Beag a chance to turn Queen's evidence – if indeed he was a member of the gang itself.

Minahan said the reward was going to be announced on 2 November, the day after the insurance claims were due to be paid and on which, technically, Lloyds and the other insurers became the majority shareholders in the missing horse.

Jaysus, I thought, it had taken long enough but it was finally there. I left Minahan's office in a state of jubilation, but I was also resolved to pass the word out to some people who mattered – just in case there were any last minute changes of heart.

My first act was to contact James Beag – using the small ad columns of the *Daily Mirror* as I had agreed. I arranged an insertion which read:

PERSONAL

J.S. The Race is on starting 2nd.

It was a natural follow up to my first message to him – inserted in the *Mirror* just before I had gone to see Drion:

PERSONAL

J. SMALL. Under orders C.T.

This had indicated that Drion was going to see me again. But unfortunately, my new communications system hit a snag I could not have foreseen. The second message did appear, but my initials were left off the end and in some newspapers the date was blurred. I complained to the *Mirror* but by the time it could be corrected Lloyds had made the formal announcement and, to my fury, I was not the first source of the information for my mystery voice. But I didn't really care. The reward was my doing. That was what mattered, and Beag would realize that.

I reinserted the *Mirror* messsage, this time making it even more clear, so that it read:

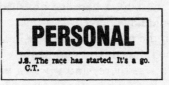

On Wednesday, 26 October, I had made a special trip to Ireland to secure my position with two of the men who were central to the investigation: Superintendent Murphy and Captain Tim Rogers. I was determined to be the source of the news that the reward was coming. It might be too late of course – there was no way of telling – but at least I had achieved what I set out to do.

Murphy's reaction was a mixed one. He was delighted for me that something was about to happen after my long battle – he had respect for my efforts even though he didn't agree fully with my aim. But he was also apprehensive. From what I had said, it was obvious to him that the syndicate had been holding out on him – which was something I had always believed anyway. His reaction as a policeman was that whatever the syndicate or the insurers did, it didn't change the nature of his investigation. He still had the criminals to catch. But he admitted to me privately that, as a horse lover, he was delighted that I had won my fight to get a bigger reward.

Rogers was also delighted for me. I told him I had flown over to Ireland especially to tell him the news, and he said he believed it was a very positive step, though he feared it had probably come too late. He said he couldn't understand why the insurers had now agreed at this late stage, when back in May, he, Rogers, had proposed to Drion that the syndicate members should contribute to a reward and they had got nowhere.

He said that he would have been sorry to take some of the glamour away from me, but he felt that if Drion had listened to him in May, he and other syndicate members would have been making the running instead of leaving it to the insurers to do it now.

Rogers' final question to me was, 'How did you get all the information you have acquired?'

I shook his hand with a smile, and said, 'I, as a journalist, never divulge my sources.'

He also asked me why I hadn't published everything in a newspaper – it could have helped.

I said no, not in the position that I was in at the time.

I was determined that this was to be the end of my involvement. The reward was there, and it was a big enough sum to attract Beag – or anyone else for that matter – but not big enough to be called a ransom. Beag knew where to go if he wanted to collect it – he was the one who had told me to see 'Astor, Butcher and Drion'. He knew about Minahan and Morgan also. He had no excuse for not going through with his offer, and I had no need to stand in the dangerous middle ground any longer.

At that point I would have liked to be able to walk away and do nothing further. But when you are as close to a situation as I had become, you realize that it is never that easy to walk away from anything you love, human or animal, and I desperately wanted to see Shergar safe and well, though there was nothing more I could usefully do.

Then, even as I was communicating the good news to Beag through the columns of the *Daily Mirror*, one of my most reliable sources told me that another meeting of the syndicate committee was going to be held in Newmarket on Wednesday, 30 November, at the offices of Ruston and Lloyd, the solicitors who had originally set up the Shergar syndicate.

As before, certain good friends allowed me to be present by proxy. I couldn't be the fly on the wall that I would have liked to have been, but the account I finally got of the meeting was almost as good.

It took place at 5 p.m. on Wednesday the 30th, with Drion in the chair, in a building which had the White Hart Hotel on one side and the cabaret club and the King Edward's Memorial Hall on the other. Most of the members of the syndicate attended that meeting and, by all accounts, some of them would have been better off performing in the cabaret next door!

A number of routine matters were dealt with. Michael O'Mahoney of McCann, Fitzgerald and Sutton, the syndicate's solicitors, said the claim by the syndicate against Kildare County Council for negligence in failing to protect Shergar was going ahead, but it would have to be held in abeyance indefinitely. He said that under the terms of the ancient law the horse would have to be proved dead, and without that evidence no action could be taken. However, he did confirm that the syndicate *was* entitled to bring the suit – it was not limited to Irish citizens as had been thought by some members.

There was also a discussion of the insurance position during which it came out that, despite the press reports and statements, no actual insurance claim had been paid out at the beginning of November. Several members, notably Lord Derby, were furious about this and were demanding tough action to force the payment of the claim. In the course of this argument it transpired that, as things stood at the moment, the insurers would end up owning technically forty-four per cent of the horse – once they had paid the claim – not the sixty per cent that had been mentioned to me by Terry Minahan.

As it happened, by Christmas the insurance brokers had, it appeared, given up hope of ever finding Shergar dead or alive. Everyone who had been involved seemed only interested in one thing: closing the book on the mystery. Terry Minahan's company had started to pay out on the theft policies and by Christmas they had paid out £3.4 million of the £4.2 million of their cover. But while the affairs of those with theft policies, as

169

far as the insurance was concerned, had been settled, this was far from the case for some of the other syndicate members who had mortality policies. With no body for identification and no proof that Shergar was dead, their battle to get back their insurance was only just beginning. Presumably some shareholders insured by other brokers are facing the same problems.

The technical adviser then stood up and made a statement. He promised the members that he would have some solid information for them in about fourteen days' time. From this, and other things he said, some shareholders understood him to mean that he had received *new* information. However, he was given a very rough ride by a number of members who said they were fed up with promises. Nothing had been delivered and they were only being told half truths. The technical adviser was then accused by some members of advising only the Aga Khan. His explanation to the meeting was that, although it was true he had been hired by the Aga Khan, he was working for him on the assumption that the syndicate was being informed by the committee of what was going on.

It was round this point that the meeting began to hot up, and some syndicate members started asking heavy, and even loaded questions. The first of these questions was put to Drion as chairman.

'Who do you think was responsible for the kidnapping of Shergar?'

I had asked some of the members to try and put this question because the Aga Khan had apparently told some syndicate members, during the running of the Prix de l'Arc de Triomphe, that the IRA had killed Shergar. Also because, sixteen days later, his stud manager, Ghislain Drion, had told me at Bally-many he believed the horse was alive.

At the Newmarket meeting, Drion's answer was bold and unequivocal. 'Most of us are of the opinion that the kidnapping was carried out by the IRA,' he said.

Immediately another member of the syndicate stood up and said, 'Monsieur Drion, a lot of bad things go on in Ireland, but I can tell you that I am completely privy to a former Prime Minister's knowledge of the situation, and neither the present government, nor the Special Branch in Dublin Castle, say the IRA did it.'

The member was asked whether he was sure of his statement. 'Yes. Positively,' he replied.

The investigator then reiterated what Drion had said – that the finger pointed towards the IRA. Several members objected strongly that such a statement should be made to the meeting without any proof being brought – especially, they said, as it clashed with their own information that the IRA was *not* the main culprit.

Shergar's vet, Stan Cosgrove, was one of those who spoke up on Drion's side. He demanded that the objectors produce their sources for saying it was not an IRA job. Naturally, no one was willing to divulge sources and, anyway, Mr Cosgrove was himself on shakey ground. He was the next to be hammered by the meeting for his role in one of the most curious of all the later mysteries surrounding the Shergar kidnap.

On 11 November, a curious and sensational story had appeared in the Irish newspapers. It said that the Garda were investigating the disappearance of £80,000-worth of ransom money, which had been about to be paid to the supposed kidnappers of Shergar in July.

According to the Irish press reports, a package containing the money, in used notes, was given by an Irish detective to a farmer in County Clare who was to act as intermediary. The farmer told the police that he left the money in the boot of a car so that it could be collected if Shergar was returned. When the farmer returned to the car, the money had vanished.

The next day, *The Times* reported the same story, adding that a team of detectives investigating the story had cleared all the police in the Shergar squad of any involvement. According to *The Times*, the money was handed over to an Irish policeman by Stan Cosgrove. The policeman was supposed to be acting as an intermediary with a third party who claimed to have information about where Shergar was. In its report of 12 November, *The Times* quoted Mr Cosgrove as saying the report was a fairytale.

'No sum was ever passed. There might have been mention of money to get back the horse but that would be as far as it would go,' Cosgrove said, according to *The Times*.

I was in Ireland at the time the report broke, doing more research, and no one took the story at face value. Because it

171

immediately came under internal police investigation, it was virtually impossible to get anyone to say anything and, for the time being at least, Mr Cosgrove's denial had to be accepted. The situation changed dramatically, however, at the Newmarket meeting.

Cosgrove was questioned by several members sitting round the table, and he admitted that he was the source of the money which was put in the boot of the car, and that it had disappeared. Amazingly, there was no uproar. As chairman, Drion was at pains to establish that Cosgrove had acted on his own initiative and the negotiations that were supposed to have been in progress when the money vanished were nothing to do with the committee. Cosgrove confirmed this. He had acted on his own, although, he said, the £80,000 had come from other members of the syndicate.

To my astonishment, no one tried to put Cosgrove on the spot. He wasn't asked who the syndicate members were, or what evidence he had received in July to make him feel it was worth risking £80,000 in reward money. He wasn't asked to explain why he hadn't briefed the other members of the syndicate or the committee.

Captain Rogers commented at the meeting that no one had ever asked him to come up with reward money – even though he had indicated he was always willing to contribute under the committee's auspices. In fact, Captain Rogers pointedly reminded Drion that on 22 May, he, Rogers, had proposed that a reward should be organized and Drion had not had the courtesy to keep his promise to come back to him on it.

Drion apologized to Rogers in front of the rest of the meeting for this failure, but still there was no further quizzing of Stan Cosgrove.

With the Irish police conducting an internal enquiry into the disappearance of the £80,000, I can see that there wasn't a great deal of room for manoeuvre left to the committee, but it still seems astonishing that this incident – so similar to my own experiences with Beag – should have been allowed to pass the committee with so little scrutiny.

If I had been at the meeting, I would have asked Drion why he hadn't informed the committee of all the information I had passed on to him, especially my belief that confidence money had been paid earlier – at the time of Beag's information concerning Flight 208. Did other syndicate members pay confidence money at that time also, without informing the committee? Indeed, were the payments in some way connected? Were they – as had been speculated – part of a series of instalments of ransom payment? Was it possible that the kidnappers had pulled a flanker on three people simultaneously: Stan Cosgrove, myself, and Captain Sean Berry, the Secretary of the Irish Thoroughbred Breeders' Association? He, too, had become involved with people who claimed to be the kidnappers, and who had approached him in much the same roundabout way as Beag had approached me.

During the early months of the kidnapping, while I was dealing with Beag, Berry had been forced to play the same games I had – with mystery voices, coded signals and trips at odd hours to public call-boxes. The timing of Berry's dealings is particularly fascinating and the approaches to him were made in two stages.

In an interview with *The Sunday Press*, he described how he received four calls between St Patrick's Day, 17 March, and 27 March. Three different voices were involved in the calls, all of them speaking with what Captain Berry described as 'cultured Irish accents'. They asked him what reward was on offer and Berry told them £100,000 – a higher figure, incidentally, than had ever been mentioned either in public or among insiders in the racing world. The callers said it wasn't enough. Raise it to £250,000 they said, and a deal might be possible. Nothing ever came of the calls, however.

This was, of course, the period when I was 'summoned' to Ireland to be looked over by James Beag's associates. The day I spent in Jury's Hotel in Dublin waiting, in a state of fury and frustration, to be given information about Shergar, was 24 March. I was told by Beag later that nothing had come of my trip because 'something had gone wrong'. Was there any connection between whatever had gone wrong and the dealings with Captain Berry? I have no way of knowing, but it certainly seems an unlikely coincidence of dates if there was no link at all.

Captain Berry says he was contacted again on 2 May, and, again, he believed the contact was promising enough for him to go to the Hotel Keadeen in Newbridge. In his interview,

Captain Berry recounts how he received another phone call while he was at the hotel, and was told he would be taken to Shergar if he brought £250,000 with him. The negotiations continued along these lines over the next few days, with Captain Berry making various trips to public call-boxes to talk to the mystery callers. Naturally enough, he insisted that he could not go anywhere with money until he had absolute proof that the horse was alive.

Despite the risk to himself, Captain Berry at one point offered to go and stay with the horse until a deal could be worked out, but nothing came of the negotiations. In Captain Berry's own words, 'They never produced evidence to me directly. I believe a picture of the horse was sent to the police, but we never had access to that.'

As he put it later in the interview: 'The Shergar trail really petered out at this point, unfortunately. There have been no further really significant calls. I cannot say why the contact broke down at that stage.'

It has to be said that if the syndicate committee had been doing its job properly, all of this information would have been pooled and a much clearer picture would have been available to members – and to the police – of what was going on. Instead, the dealings that Berry, Cosgrove and I have had remain unanswered questions in an apparently endless series.

The first and most obvious question which the whole world asked was did the IRA really kidnap and perhaps cause the death of Shergar? Clearly the possibility can't be ruled out but, in my own judgement, there was a doubt about it. If it was a normal IRA job, why did they never claim responsibility for it? Not to do so is completely out of character. The IRA has claimed responsibility for some of the most outrageous atrocities, so why would they stop short of admitting they had killed Shergar? I make the speculation with some confidence because, throughout my own investigations, my police contacts – who have proved extremely reliable in the past – have told me they believe the IRA was involved only marginally.

My belief – backed up by some information I have been receiving from the police – is that the kidnapping was the work of an international gang helped by the IRA. I think the IRA has kept quiet about their role not out of shame, but because they acted on behalf of someone else – some organization which was providing them with arms or money, and which has insisted on their silence.

This leads to the next question. Why did the 'official' ransom demands end so soon after Shergar's disappearance? Was it – as was speculated at the time – because the horse was killed, or because he died in an accident four days after the kidnap? Again, this has to be treated as a possibility, but all of my dealings with Beag and with other key figures in the situation – including Monsieur Drion – made me believe otherwise.

If I need support for this view, I have only to look at the dealings which Cosgrove and Berry undertook in the middle of the summer, since it seems to me incredible that *they* would have been completely taken in by hoaxers. We should also ask why Drion himself believed the horse was alive as late as 17 October.

So how important a part of the kidnap was the ransom? If Shergar is alive and it was not a kidnap for ransom, what was the motive? Was it revenge – a theft carried out by someone who had a personal grudge against the Aga Khan? Right from the beginning, the press suggested there were a number of people within the racing industry who fitted the bill. The only one who was ever named was the American breeder, Wayne Murty, who described himself as the most obvious suspect – while at the same time strongly denying that he had actually taken the horse, even though he admitted having once *considered* doing so.

Murty was ruled out quite quickly both by the police and by private enquiries, but there were others in racing who might hate the Aga Khan enough to want to humiliate him by stealing a prize possession.

I must also allow that religion could have played a part in the disappearance of Shergar. The Aga Khan is the spiritual leader of about twelve million Muslims, and has political *and* religious enemies – notably the Libyan leader, Colonel Gaddafi, once described as 'Africa's unguided missile'.

In the course of my investigations both North and South of the border, his name came up several times, to the point where I had mentioned him both to Drion and to Superintendent Murphy. Gaddafi is particularly well equipped for a venture like the Shergar kidnapping because of his known support for the IRA and his direct links with them and other international terrorist

175

organizations. He would have the expertise to carry it out – and the motive, in his hatred of the Aga Khan – but his name has never figured centrally in the police investigations.

There are unanswered questions, too, about the role of the Irish Government. The Government was involved from the very first hours of the kidnapping when Finance Minister, Alan Dukes, was one of the first people to be informed and contacted Justice Minister, Michael Noonan. Yet the Government seems to have been strangely reticent in its handling of the Shergar affair.

The questions the Irish people themselves have raised are: why has the Government been silent? Why has it made no statements on the kidnapping? Why has it allowed a Mickey Mouse investigation to drag on, when the affair is damaging the bloodstock industry, which is worth one hundred million pounds to the country?

'Mickey Mouse' is the only way to describe an investigation which quickly saw the team of forty detectives reduced to a handful by 24 April, because the authorities had decided that the cost of the ten-week enquiry had run over budget. This criticism in no way detracts from the respect and admiration I have for Superintendent Jimmy Murphy and his team, but after the cut back they were operating under incredible handicaps. Not the least of these was the fact that there were no funds for lighting and heating in the police caravan at Ballymany, and the officers had to go out and buy candles!

It certainly seemed to the Irish public that the police weren't getting very enthusiastic backing from the Irish Government. Was the Government reluctant to act because of the international make-up of the syndicate – did they feel it couldn't be treated as a straightforward Irish matter? Was this something which made them hesitate to pursue the investigation vigorously? Was it the theory that the kidnapping might have been a personal act of vengeance against the Aga Khan by the Libyan leader, Colonel Gaddafi, that made the Government want to play down the whole situation as much as possible?

Until October 1983, the Irish police had one of the best reputations in Europe for handling kidnap situations. In the last few years ten kidnappings have taken place in Ireland and every one of them has resulted in a victory for the police. The kidnap victims have all been released alive, though in a number of cases ransom demands and small rewards have been paid. The only advantage that the police have got out of the Shergar affair thus far is that they have a lever to use on any gang – particularly any IRA gang – that they happen to be after. When gang members are pulled in for questioning, one of the first things they will have to prove to the police is that they were *not* involved in the kidnapping of Shergar!

The question that the overall handling of the Shergar case raises is why was this kidnap different? Was it simply because it concerned an animal and not a human being?

How could people, no matter how rich they are, just dismiss the whole kidnapping of such a beautiful horse as Shergar? Some, it seems, were even willing to accept the situation without doing anything whatsoever to try to recover the animal. They wrote Shergar off, as though he were a used match.

Their reasons for not paying a *ransom* might well be justified, but their failure to organize a proper *reward* is inexcusable. Right from the first moment when Beag called me on 12 February, my aim was to get the syndicate, and later the insurers, to put up a decent reward to entice a weak link in the gang to come out and unravel the mystery. I believed then – and I still believe now – that £100,000 or £150,000 could have achieved this.

But I also condemn the Aga Khan and the syndicate for failing to handle the affair properly. In kidnap situations, whether they concern human beings or animals, the lines of communication must always be kept open. Successes are achieved by negotiation, by keeping the kidnappers talking, by encouraging anyone who might have information to come out with it. Not by building walls of silence and closing off any openings which appear, in order to save face.

I would have expected the syndicate to be prepared to make some kind of deal with Beag – or indeed with any of the others who tried to contact them – both to get the horse back and to save from embarrassment the Irish and British Governments, the Aga Khan, the shareholders, even the stable staff at Ballymany and at other stud farms throughout Ireland. It's almost impossible to describe to an outsider just how great this embarrassment was.

177

People were embarrassed not so much by the kidnapping as by the wheeling and dealing that went on after it. Even Shergar's groom, Jimmy Fitzgerald, and his family, for instance, were hidden away, stripped of all dignity.

People both high and low, and ordinary members of the Irish public and wealthy members of the syndicate all felt insulted that they were told so little about it. I encountered some owners who were ashamed to admit they were members of the Shergar syndicate because they disapproved so much of the way the kidnap was being handled. No one seemed to know what was happening.

I am sure this embarrassment could well have been avoided if the lines of communication had been kept open and a realistic reward offered. Now people are concerned to look for scapegoats – like Superintendent Jimmy Murphy and, perhaps in the long run, Ghislain Drion himself.

But at least the reward is there now. I want to believe – indeed, I have to believe – that it is still not too late. The thought that I might eventually persuade the parties concerned to put up a reward sustained me through the worst days of the investigation. It has taken a long time but a decent reward is finally available and I remain convinced that it is the one thing which could still lead to the recovery of the horse.

James Beag may yet be the man who claims it, but if he doesn't, there must still be people out there somewhere with valuable information. From the outset, people have been afraid to talk. As I am writing now, neither the police nor anyone else knows the exact extent of IRA involvement. Nevertheless, ordinary Irish people feel that they *must* be involved in some way and that belief alone has been enough to keep mouths tightly closed. It takes a lot to overcome that fear but who knows – perhaps the £250,000 reward I have worked so hard to raise might just be enough.

Author's Epilogue

On 9 October I received my last telephone call from the man who had come into my life from nowhere. The question that will haunt me for the rest of my life is, 'Who was Beag?' Why did he pick on me and what was his part in the whole Shergar mystery? There is no doubt in my mind now that Beag, or whatever his real name is, was a member of the gang who helped to steal Shergar. No one else could have known so much.

I make no claims to be a professional investigator and I make no apologies either for any mistakes I have made. I am sure there are dozens of questions you would have liked me to have asked, and you may have wondered sometimes why I didn't force the issues, particularly with Beag, or Drion, or the insurance people. Let me be frank: I often held back because of concern for my own safety. One of my objects – and I'm not ashamed to admit it – was to emerge with my own skin as intact as possible!

Looking back over those months, there were times when I was scared out of my life about it all, but the funny thing now is that I never really had any fear of Beag. I played it straight down the line with him – though I didn't always tell him things immediately or when I should have done. I kept him as near to the situation as he had asked me to get. I found him pleasant and understanding most of the time. He sounded like someone who would ask a few questions first, before doing something.

I know that one day I will be standing in a hotel or bar somewhere in the world and Beag will be standing right beside me. He knows me, but I never saw him. I don't know what he looks like, even though I have built up a picture of him. I recall one day when Jimmy Murphy asked me about him.

'What do you think he's like? From his voice and his manner

and so on, on the phone?'

'I think he's like anyone, maybe a bit like the two of us. Maybe he's got my looks, and your brains. He is the complete mystery man,' I told Murphy.

How and where was he making those phone calls? Sometimes I could hear noise in the background, and I know that he had something clamped over the mouthpiece of the phone. One big worry I had was what I would do if I discovered him in the call-box next to me! I used to look around, to see if I could see anyone who looked like him. But then I told myself not to be so foolish – how would you know a mystery man?

Trying to explain to other people – like the police and even members of the syndicate and the insurance underwriters – that I was talking to a man who was only a voice left me feeling very foolish most of the time. It was embarrassing. How do you explain something like that? You feel a 'right eejit', as we would say in Ireland.

Beag was a big chip on my shoulder. I know that, at the time, I couldn't go anywhere without thinking about him. I still think about him now. After I suggested that all our future dealings should be done through the newspapers, that was it. I suppose I'll never know who he was. But I have kept my promise to Beag. I have written this book, which tells the story as it was at the time. If you are out there, Beag, and reading this, you know I'm telling it as it was – the truth.

The horse was my main concern. Dead or alive, I wanted Shergar back. Alive to live and enjoy the green pastures of the country fields in the land where he and I were born. Dead, if it has to be, he should be given a true resting place beside the racecourse at the Curragh. Shergar's history cannot be written until he is found, and until more people tell what they know. Unlike us, Shergar never knew how to cheat and deceive or be unkind. We know all these things. Shergar didn't.

Shergar

Shergar, by Great Nephew out of Sharmeen, was born at the Aga Khan's Sheshoon Stud in Co. Kildare in 1978.

This bay colt had a quiet beginning, and after twelve months was sent to the Beech Hurst Stable, Newmarket, which is owned by trainer Michael Stoute.

Michael Stoute was born in 1945 and, from his early entry into the Sport of Kings, was very eager to learn everything about racing and showed that he was a man with a golden touch. He eventually became one of the trainers picked by the Aga Khan to look after some of his horses in Britain.

Shergar took well to the racing scene, on the Bury Road at Newmarket under the care of Stoute, and looked just like a normal sort of bay colt. He didn't show anything on the gallops, but his owner, the Aga Khan, was hoping that with his background he could become a nice miler.

While Stoute continued to train the colt, another member of the Shergar 'family', jockey Walter Swinburn, was making his way in the sport. Born in 1961, young Walter came into a family who lived, slept and dreamed horses. His mother was from a great Irish horse family, and his father, Wally, was the champion jockey in Ireland.

After his schooling in Ireland – where he was looked on as a future football or rugby player – horses were never far away. He finished school a little early and was sent to the famous Frenchie Nicholson Jockey's Apprentice School to learn his trade. On 12 July 1978, just a few months after Shergar was born, Walter Swinburn rode his first winner – Paddy's Luck – at Kempton Park.

But it was Lester Piggott who was to team up with Shergar for *his* first race on 19 September 1980 at Newbury, where he won

181

the Kris Plate over one mile, winning £2,560 for his owner. On 25 October Shergar had his second race, in the William Hill Futurity Stakes at Doncaster, also over a mile. After another good performance, he lost to Beldale Flutter by two and a half lengths. This was his only other race as a two-year-old.

Over the winter the colt improved considerably, but not many punters or experts had been impressed by his two runs the previous season. All that was to change very quickly. In his first run as a three-year-old, on 25 April 1981 in the Guardian Classic Trial at Sandown Park, Shergar started at very generous odds, and to say he slammed a good field may still be an understatement. He beat one of the well-fancied runners, Kirtling, by ten lengths. This time Shergar was ridden by Walter Swinburn, who was getting to know the colt. After that win the punters and racing press were quietly talking about his having a good chance in the Derby.

The Aga Khan and Michael Stoute could now see the potential in their runner and, with the Derby definitely in mind, they planned the next stage of their campaign. Shergar's final run before the Epsom Derby was in the Chester Vase over ten furlongs. On 5 May a big crowd gathered at Chester, and they were all looking forward to a pretty tight race. But what they got was another brilliant display from the colt. He had killed off the opposition before the furlong pole and, under a gentle ride from Walter Swinburn, Shergar won the Chester Vase by twelve lengths.

After that excellent win he was installed as the favourite for the Derby. Beldale Flutter, the only horse that had inflicted defeat on Shergar, and winner of the Mecca Dante at York, had suffered a set back when he was in a freak accident with one of the great sprint horses we had in the country, Moorestyle. The one horse that might have tested Shergar was now out of the Derby on 3 June.

But there was no doubt that Shergar had come from being an inexperienced two-year-old to an outstanding three-year-old. He dominated all the headlines leading up to the race, even after the decision by Lester Piggott to ride Shotgun, who had finished second to Beldale Flutter in the Mecca Dante. The only doubt the experts had didn't concern the horse but was about how jockey Walter Swinburn would handle the situation. At nineteen, he was the youngest jockey ever to ride the favourite for the Blue Riband of the sport. Shergar started the race at 11-10 on.

After half a mile Riberetto was the leader of the nineteen-runner field. Silver Season was close up to the leader, but after coming down the hill and rounding Tattenham Corner, Shergar was given his head. Swinburn slackened the reins a little and, as one punter said afterwards, 'He just flew'. He accelerated away and, even though Walter Swinburn eased up before the post, Shergar won the 1981 Epsom Derby by ten lengths. It was the widest winning margin in the Derby's history. Glint of Gold, owned by Paul Mellon, finished second, with Scintillating Air third and Lester Piggott on Shotgun fourth.

After that Derby win Shergar had won all his three races as a three-year-old and the total winning margin in the three was over thirty-two lengths. His next race was to be the Irish Sweeps Derby at the Curragh in Ireland, just across the road from where he was born, and on 27 June Shergar was reunited with Lester Piggott after Walter Swinburn was suspended by the Stewards at Royal Ascot. But Swinburn was in the crowd to see Shergar win his second Derby – this time by a shorter four lengths.

The King George the Sixth and Queen Elizabeth Diamond Stakes was the next target, and with Walter Swinburn now back on board a fascinating race was in prospect – this was the first time that Shergar would face older horses. Walter got trapped along the rail, but Light Cavalry, one of the front runners, got tired, moved out and allowed Walter on Shergar to come up the inside. With a clear run he flew past Master Willie to land his fifth successive win of the season. The Aga Khan and Michael Stoute said they would aim Shergar for the Prix de L'Arc de Triomphe at Longchamp in October.

Somewhere between victory in the King George and the run-up to the Arc, someone changed their mind. Shergar was entered for the St Leger at Doncaster, but no one thought he would go there because it was too soon before the richest race in Europe. Shergar *did* go to Doncaster for the St Leger on 12 September, however, and, in very heavy conditions, the colt got bogged down in the mud and could only manage to finish fourth behind Cut Above. So ended the racing career of Shergar. In all he had had eight races. He won six and collected over £320,000 in prize money for his owner.

He was offered out to syndication and thirty-three shares were sold to other racing men and organizations, to join the Aga Khan in the ownership of Shergar at stud. Every nomination to Shergar cost £80,000. Normally, part of that fee is paid when the mating takes place and the second part when it's confirmed that the mare is in foal, but with Shergar the deal was that the whole of the £80,000 was to be paid up front.

In his first year he was given to forty mares and from them came thirty-five foals. His first offspring, a colt, was born to an American mare, Hilo Girl, owned by the millionaire Bertram Firestone (who had one share in Shergar at stud). A second colt, named Lot 303, was the first of Shergar's foals to go on sale. At public auction at Goff's Bloodstock Sales Centre in Co. Kildare on 20 November 1983, and after some spirited bidding, the colt was sold for 260,000 guineas.

Shergar's Pedigree

SHERGAR b. 1978			
Great Nephew b. 1963	Honeyway	Fairway	Phalaris
			Scapa Flow
		Honey Buzzard	Papyrus
			Lady Peregrine
	Sybil's Niece	Admiral's Walk	Hyperion
			Tabaris
		Sybil's Sister	Nearco
			Sister Sarah
Sharmeen b. 1972	Val de Loir	Vieux Manoir	Brantôme
			Vieille Maison
		Vali	Sunny Boy
			Her Slipper
	Nasreen	Charlottesville	Prince Chevalier
			Noorani
		Ginetta	Tulyar
			Diableretta